Primary Education \

CW00742220

Over the past two years, the *Primary Education Voices* podcast has welcomed dozens of inspirational educators with a variety of roles across primary education to share what they are passionate about. This book gives some of these educators the chance to discuss their ideas, research and reflections in a more in-depth manner to help the reader reflect more deeply about their own practice.

This publication is a collation of writing of incredible philosophies, resources and ideas from primary practitioners, for primary practitioners. Engaging chapters cover a wide range of topics for the contributors of this book to share: from developing the right ethos and culture in your school or classroom, to considering how to make your curriculum more rich and inclusive, to considering how to look after your own well-being and vitality in the role of a primary educator. Within each chapter, you will hear from a number of contributors and be given the space to reflect on what they have shared, along with some thought-provoking questions to prompt you on how to adapt and refine your practice.

These ideas and insights will be essential to all who work within the primary sector including trainees, early career teachers and middle and senior leaders, as well as all those who support and consult with these individuals who seek to change and improve their practice.

Matt Roberts is a primary school teacher, currently in Year 6, and is KS2, Maths, Curriculum, and Assessment Lead. He hosts and produces the *Primary Education Voices* podcast which shares a platform for inspirational primary colleagues to share what they are passionate about in Primary Education.

Primary Education Voices

Matt Roberts

Routledge
Taylor & Francis Group

LONDON AND NEW YORK

Designed cover image: insspirito via Pixaby

First published 2024
by Routledge
4 Park Square, Milton Park, Abingdon, Oxon, OX14 4RN

and by Routledge
605 Third Avenue, New York, NY 10158

Routledge is an imprint of the Taylor & Francis Group, an informa business

© 2024 Matt Roberts

British Library Cataloguing-in-Publication Data
A catalogue record for this book is available from the British Library

ISBN: 978-1-032-30890-6 (hbk)
ISBN: 978-1-032-30891-3 (pbk)
ISBN: 978-1-003-30715-0 (ebk)

DOI: 10.4324/9781003307150

Typeset in Bembo and Helvetica Neue
by KnowledgeWorks Global Ltd.

Contents

List of contributors

*@MrKAdams_*

At his previous school, Kyrome Adams was English Lead (Writing and Reading). Reading is something that he is extremely passionate about. He was also Computing Lead and regularly told staff to turn their devices on and off when they had a problem, TES columnist, and probably best known for his viral FootShake dance. He is currently a Year 6 teacher and Phase 3 Leader at The Halifax Academy so he is responsible for Years 5, 6, and 7. He also has self-published a book called "My Daddy Changed the World," which is about the discrimination a black person may face written for children to help them understand these injustices and to aid important conversations through pictures.

@etaknipsa

Kate Aspin has been in Primary teaching since 1994, working in the north of England, Lancashire, Manchester, Calderdale, and Kirklees. She has been a Deputy and FT class teacher (juggle, juggle) and then Acting Head three times. Now she works in ITT, teaching, and supporting Primary QTS trainees from undergraduates to PGCE, SCITT, apprenticeships, and School Direct. Kate is also a vice chair of a local primary school and still supply teachers when she is able, to keep her hand in and remember what it is all for.

@katebodle

Kate Bodle has worked in a variety of state primary school and college settings as a teacher and also a trainer of specialist dyslexia teachers. She is now Deputy Head of a small independent primary school with responsibilities including SENDCo, Pastoral and Wellbeing lead, and DSL. Her driving purpose within all her roles is to ensure that every child is enabled to fulfil not only his/her potential but also his/her passions by ensuring barriers to learning are minimised. Kate finds this works best by training and utilising adults around the child to ensure consistency and support through meaningful relationships.

@ClareCampbell7

Dr Clare Campbell is the mum of two teenage boys, an executive Headteacher and author of eight books for teachers. She has an MA in SEND and a doctorate in education. She has lectured at MMU, Manchester University, Liverpool Hope and Tangaza University in Nairobi. She has been working in education since 1999 and has taught all age groups from EY to KS3. She is passionate about learning environments and trauma-informed practice, spirituality and the arts.

@HappyHead74

Victoria Carr is a mum, Headteacher, Reserve Officer in the Intelligence Corps, Chartered Manager, author, and TEDx speaker. She advocates that there is a social imperative for those in leadership positions to actively create opportunities for transformational interactions with others. She has two MAs: one in Equality and Diversity, the other in Leadership and has just completed a third MA in Military History. Her doctorate is in leadership and politics in the educational domain. She is already working on her second book on School Improvement.

@MrEFinch

Ed Finch is the principal at Chagford Primary School in the heart of the Dartmoor National Park. Ed is also co-founder of #BrewEd, bringing educators together for pints and pedagogy since 2017. Together with Daryn Simon, Ed was named one of the TES top ten most influential educators in 2019. Ed is passionate about life, love and stories.

@TJGriffiths

Tom Griffiths is the Assistant Headteacher at Tidbury Green School in Solihull. Some of his current roles include Maths lead, staff governor, curriculum coach, and DSL. He has previously worked in inner-city schools in London and Nottingham. Tom also blogs about children's books at Check 'Em Out Books and tweets @TJGriffiths.

@TeacherPaul1978

Paul Hume qualified to teach in 2007 and has taught in a wide range of primary schools throughout London. He is currently Deputy Headteacher at a West-London bilingual primary school.

Children's resilience, independence, and well-being are his aim as a teacher, but he is also committed to making sure teachers' workload is reduced, and ultimately their well-being is looked after. To relax, you might find him running around the parks and river trails or snuggled up on the sofa with a film or book.

@richreadsalot

Rich Simpson has worked in a variety of roles in Primary Education for 23 years and currently works as an Acting Head of School. He has a love for using books in teaching and learning, sharing regular blogs and updates about relevant quality texts for use in education. He runs the weekly #kindnessripple on Thursdays and #SwitchOffSaturday and is passionate about supporting teachers' well-being.

@smithsmm

Simon Smith has been working in education for 29 years, predominantly as a teacher but for the last 8 years as a Headteacher. He has mainly worked in schools with significant disadvantages in the North East of England and has seen the impact great teaching can have on the opportunities pupils have. He is passionate about the transformative power of books in education and especially the value of picture books in helping start children on the journey to become lifelong readers and to open pupils' eyes to the world around them.

@kyrstiestubbs

Kyrstie Stubbs currently works as Deputy CEO for INSPIRE partnership MAT supporting nine primary schools across Wakefield and Pontefract. Previously, she worked as a Headteacher across two very different schools in West Yorkshire leading both from RI to Good and her last school obtained outstanding across two areas. Supporting and celebrating diversity and equity has been her passion in all her roles. She hopes by contributing to this book she can make a difference to others by supporting them through their own journey to this aim.

@TsuiAllen

Allen Tsui is the subject lead for Computing at Willow Brook Primary School Academy in North East London where he has held the role since Summer 2020. Allen is also the Community Leader for the Computing at School Waltham Forest Mixed Community. Willow Brook is part of the Griffin Schools Trust, a family of twelve schools, three of which are in East London. Allen is a certified Professional

Development Leader and has completed the hat-trick of certificates awarded by the DfE-funded National Centre for Computing Education to teach Computing at Primary and Secondary standards. Allen is very prolific on Twitter: @TsuiAllen

@priscigeeks

Bryony Turford is passionate about professional learning and has many roles supporting teachers across Yorkshire and beyond including: Chartered Science Teacher (CSciTeach); Senior Regional Hub Leader for PSQM, Red Kite Primary CPD lead, and regional trainer for CLEAPSS. She is part of the author team for the Snap Science series, co-author of 100 ideas for Primary Science and has written many chapters and articles for a range of publications including ASE Primary Science. She is also a member of the ASE Futures committee and an active member of ASE. Since 2021, Bryony has been working alongside Paul Tyler, to create and run My Science Club. An online resource for educators looking to enhance science provision beyond the classroom.

@PaulWat5

Paul Watson trained at Bradford College before starting his teaching career in his home town of Hartlepool. Thereafter, he moved to schools in Sunderland and Middlesbrough. His extensive experience in leading areas of curriculum and three outstanding Ofsteds to date are appearing useful as he is currently starting out on his Headteacher journey at Thorntree Academy.

@pennywpennyw

Penny Whelan is a Primary Assistant Headteacher and SENCO. She has a Psychology degree and a PGCE. Penny works part-time and is also an EAL coordinator, an SLE, Coach, and the Operations Manager for the Schools Linking Network in her Local Authority. She is passionate about SEND, inclusion, community, and diversity.

@adamjames317

Adam Woodward is a teacher based in Kent who is passionate about teaching and learning, curriculum, and teacher development. He has been a teacher for 15 years with various roles across both the state and independent sectors and is currently the Lead Teacher at a school in Bexley. Adam has spoken about the implementation of knowledge organisers in primary schools at several ResearchED conferences and has recently had his thoughts on this subject published as a case study in Kate Jones' "Retrieval Practice: Primary" book.

@OliverSLT

Oliver Wright lives in Sheffield and has worked in primary education for over 25 years. His experience ranges from large city to small Peak District schools, including 8 years of headship in two very different settings. During his time in school, he led a whole range of developments from curriculum design, use of new technology, and improving teaching and learning to improving engagement with parents and large-scale building projects as well as looking after the thousand-and-one tasks involved in the day-to-day running of a school. He now supports those who lead, engages in school improvement work, and is a school governor.

Introduction

Matt Roberts

I didn't always want to be a teacher. However, I just loved primary school. My friends were there, every day fuelled my love of learning, and school events excited me (class assemblies, school trips, sports days – anything)! I think the thing that I loved most about primary school was the variety. One moment I was inspired to be a future author; weaving prose and verbiage together or stringing a collection of carefully crafted poetic forms together. The next moment I was excited to get stuck into mathematical theory and solve problems that perhaps I would never find myself in (I mean, whoever has that many oranges?) but it was still a sense of satisfaction when I found the solution. Then, the afternoon brought a plethora of things I could be engaged in creating my attempts at being an artist, studying the local area or far-flung continents, analysing historical evidence or experimenting with the wonders of the universe in scientific investigations. I was enthralled.

The defining moment for me was Year 6 – it was probably the best year in my education and that was in no small part down to my Year 6 teacher. They were funny, they broke things down into small steps, they were enthusiastic about every subject they taught, they found ways to provide interest in every activity, they got involved in school life; they were inspiring. I left primary school with a heavy heart and early on into Year 7 the question was suggested about what may we want to do in the future and one thing resounded clearly – primary school teacher.

Perhaps it was this Year 6 teacher and the joy he brought to the classroom in that year, perhaps it was my love of engaging in a variety of subject areas rather than focusing on one area to specialise in (yes, even my love of Maths wore thin when reaching A Level) or perhaps it was simply the brilliant memories that I left that school with. All I knew was that the decisions I made over the following seven years were directed towards my completing a BA Hons degree course in Primary Education.

Then, during this course, further inspiration hits. I was introduced to the world of edu-Twitter. I certainly didn't catch the vision of the possibilities to begin with. I interacted with a few fellow primary practitioners but very soon my NQT year began and many of those online opportunities took a backseat whilst I grappled with getting used to the life of a teacher. Despite this, every now and then I would dip my toe back in this evolving, informative world and find more and more interesting and helpful teachers out there who were sharing their expertise.

A few years later, I also fell in love with something else that was helping me to learn whilst navigating a busy life full of family, school, and other commitments – podcasts. Anyone who wants to know me just needs to look at my list of podcasts that I subscribe to and you will understand what makes me tick! As time went on, I once again became more involved on Twitter and a spark of inspiration hit me! I love communicating on Twitter with these inspirational colleagues, they have so much to share – but there is only so much that can be said in 280 characters. Not to mention the brilliant convenience that comes with podcasts that can be consumed absolutely anywhere whilst you travel or complete menial tasks that have to be done. I looked for podcasts about education (lots of them) but I wanted something that completely focused on primary education and had a variety of voices – the loud and the quiet – that were given the opportunity to share their insights into this brilliant profession. As such, Primary Education Voices was born.

Honestly, if nobody else listened to the podcast I would still have commenced this journey. I have learned an incredible amount from the incredible voices that have graced the podcast and even if I hadn't taken away the notes that I have for my own practice, just the sheer inspiration from these individuals is an incredible gift enough.

Whilst on the podcast, the guests are invited to consider what their "Primary Three" are. The "Primary Three" are three of the most important philosophies, resources, or pieces of advice that the guest would give to any primary practitioner. What I love about the "Primary Three" is that each guest is completely unique and whilst there may be similar vibes or points made by different people, the tapestry of their individual experiences paints a completely different piece of art every time each podcast recording ends. People may disagree with some views of some guests but alternative views help us consider our position and strengthen our perspective as we see other sides of the discussion.

After having interviewed dozens of these guests (who have all been recommended by other primary practitioners), I couldn't help feeling like some of the discussions that we held had to be explored further. The podcast does have a limit on how much we can discuss things and so the idea of diving deeper into a certain aspect of the conversations we had seemed like the logical next step – and that is what you are reading now.

This book will seek to take the views of guests already interviewed on Primary Education Voices, pick out one particular aspect of what they spoke about, and invite them to share more deeply their thoughts and ideas around this topic. This work will be organised into ten thematic chapters and these contributions will be grouped together so you can dive deeply with them into these areas that can easily be returned to. As there are always resources or further materials from these podcasts that people are recommended to follow, you will find plans, materials or further reading in most of these sections and along with this, some reflective questions that you can use to explore your own thinking and development in these areas.

As you read going forward, any sections that have been submitted by our fantastic contributors in their own will be in the following font:

This sentence is an example of what text from one of our wonderful contributors looks like.

This will be helpful as there will be points that I share some of my insights, additional information and summaries of what each contributor writes about. I couldn't help it – perhaps it is the keen podcaster/interviewer in me!

This work would not be possible without the valuable contributions of these brilliant primary educators. I am deeply grateful not only for the time they took to come onto the Primary Education Voices podcast but also for their generosity in sharing their incredible expertise and insights in an area that they are passionate about. I encourage you to seek them out on Twitter if you haven't already connected, and I'm sure they would welcome more opportunities to collaborate and share their vision of the future of primary education with you.

1

Ethos and attitudes

Oliver Wright – @OliverSLT
Matt Roberts – @Mroberts90Matt (drawn from
@chrisdysonHT materials)

In asking dozens and dozens of primary colleagues in a large variety of roles what the most important things about Primary Education are, a large number referred to the ethos and attitudes in the classroom. You will not get very far in maximising the potential of teaching and learning that takes place if the ethos and attitude are not attuned to being ready to learn. The two contributors to this section are all seasoned leaders who shared some great insights into the keys to building the ideal ethos in a school and therefore in your classrooms.

After all, if the ethos is correct in the microcosms that are our individual classrooms, then the school as a whole will benefit from this direction. To learn more about this vital aspect of primary education, we will first hear from Oliver Wright, who has a wide range of experience in teaching and leadership. He will share insights into what ethos means and how you can build the ethos you desire into your class or school. Then, I will share lessons learnt from a discussion with Chris Dyson, inspirational headteacher at Parklands Primary in Leeds, as a case study into how to implement the ethos you see for your class or school.

Developing ethos and values in the classroom

Oliver Wright

Spend more than a few minutes with anyone working in education and the word "ethos" will no doubt feature in the conversation. It's almost a test of whether you're a real teacher. If you can be a part of the conversation, drop in a few of the

DOI: 10.4324/9781003307150-1

key phrases and not let on that you don't have a full understanding, then you've probably passed the first test. But what exactly is ethos (and why does it matter)?

At its most basic, ethos means character and is used to describe the beliefs or ideals of a community. It's the climate within a school, something that can be sensed but is often difficult to pin down. When it's good, you know it's there. It comes through everything and just "feels" right. If there are issues, it's often difficult to work out what the problem is or what needs to be done to "fix" it. It's one of those things that good leaders understand and good educators value. They spend time creating and cultivating the "right" ethos. To an outsider, it can be a little confusing. We all work in education. We all want the best for our children. What else is there to think about?

Scratch a little deeper and a whole range of views become apparent. The best for our children can be interpreted as the best exam results, the most well-adjusted individuals, those who contribute to the greater good, those with emotional intelligence, those with high aspirations, those who are happy …. The list goes on. The only surprise here is how different all of these are.

Whatever your viewpoint, you are probably much clearer on your values than you think. What is important to you? What gets you excited? What motivates you in your work? Why do you teach? These will probably be easy questions to answer. Develop them further by asking why to each answer. So you want to see children develop confidence. That's great, but why? What impact does this have on their lives, on the lives of those around them? This can help you drill down into what exactly is important to you (and why!). This doesn't have to be an exact match to the ethos of your school, but there must be a reasonable overlap. If you're going to be happy at school, you need to believe in and be heading in the same direction as everyone else.

Even though values can vary significantly from teacher to teacher or school to school, there are some that will be core to everyone. Developing a strong ethos within your classroom is one of the joys of working in a school.

But how do we do it?

Being clear on your own values is an important starting place. If you're a bit hazy, then spend some time getting clarity on this. Keep drilling down and asking why.

Sometimes we can gain clarity on our values by exploring the times we feel out of sorts, out of place or just downright frustrated. Unpicking what it is that frustrates us or makes us unhappy about a situation can be a good indication of what is important to us (and the underlying values that stem from this).

The opposite of this is simply to look at what gives us joy. What do we enjoy doing? When are we happiest? What's on our bucket list (and why)? It can also be useful to ask those we are close to about this. They will see you as you really are. They will know your joys, sweet spots and frustrations. Quiz them and encourage feedback. Those who know us best will have a good idea of what makes us tick and the values that underpin this.

It can also be helpful from examining our bucket list of desires, to begin putting together our own personal vision statement. This can be like an aspirational manifesto for ourselves. Considering the best version of ourselves is important, but examining why this is what we aspire to and why this is important to us is even more valuable.

Often whatever threads start to become evident during this process will need to be developed further. This is where the continuing "why" questions are so helpful. Much has been written about the "5 Whys" method of questioning. In fact, the number isn't so important. What matters is drilling down and continuing to ask "why."

So, you believe that school sport should be all about everyone taking part and enjoying it.

Why?

Because children who enjoy exercise at school are more likely to go on to continue enjoying exercise in later life.

Why is this important?

Because we are preparing children for a healthy and active adulthood.

Why is this important?

Because happy and fulfilled individuals make a positive contribution to society.

What do we value?

Developing others to find their sweet spot in the world.

Now many of us will have different answers to these whys. Some of us might need to drill down even further for something really personal to us, rather than the more general (easy) answers. However long it takes and however deep we need to go, it's definitely worth it. Being clear on our values can help to steer us towards situations, opportunities or responsibilities that are where we will excel. It can also help us to avoid situations where we will be uncomfortable or struggle to thrive.

Once we're clear on values, begin to consider our class.

Everyone Counts

When it comes to ethos, everyone matters. In any class, there will be those you find it easier to get on with, harder to reach, more engaged, quieter, louder …. It's what makes working with a range of people interesting. But when it comes to ethos everyone counts! Everyone needs to be included. Everyone needs to be valued. Even if you have to work harder to include or to reach some.

It's also important that everyone knows that they are included and valued too. It's so easy for us to assume that we have communicated everything clearly. Often it needs to be stated, re-stated and gone over in a number of different ways. Communicating this truth is never finished either. It continues throughout our time with people. It needs revisiting often.

We are what we live

Much of what we communicate is unspoken. People are very good at spotting the signs that give clues to our real intentions. Telling our class that we value everyone, that we treat everyone with respect and that we try to show kindness in all situations may be important. The real test, however, is what our class sees around the edges. How do we treat others when we're in a rush, when the pressure is on, when we're juggling a few too many responsibilities or when we think no one is watching? How we treat visitors to the classroom, how we treat our cleaner and how we interact with others around the school are all telltale signs of how we really are inside. Others notice these signs and they often communicate our intentions loud and clear. Taking the time for those who need it. A few kind words. Holding that door open. That kind smile. All of these things add up to be what we're about. If we talk about compassion, understanding and a desire to help others and back that up with actions in line with our words, then people see. Even if we don't want them to, they judge us by our actions.

Small things matter

Whilst there are times that people will remember the grand gestures, the carefully planned whole school events, the impactful assemblies … often it will be the small things that stick with them. The almost unnoticed kind smile. The moment you had time for a kind word. The thought you put into dealing with a situation carefully. The time you took for people. These small things are noticed. They build up a picture of who we are. They add momentum to a positive ethos. These small almost insignificant actions are the foundations for the ethos you are trying to create. Each one is like a tiny building block, many will only be significant for an individual or small group, but the combined effect across a large group of people is significant. They are a testament to your character and influence those around you.

Have a plan

Developing a positive ethos doesn't happen by accident. Planning is important. Planning how to unpack your values. Planning how to communicate how important these values are. Planning time to come together. Planning activities to demonstrate the importance of the values. To enable people to connect with each other in a meaningful way. To demonstrate the values in action. To deepen their connection. This takes time. It takes an unwavering desire to see it happen and it takes a careful plan. As a skilful educator, you will be able to put this together. Give time to explore important concepts. Give time for learning, for change, for adaptation, for meaning. It can't be rushed. When you see a new class or new staff team come together, you can see the beginning of the creation of a great ethos in the first few days. This is definitely not something that's finished at the end of the first week though. Often, it's never finished. Often it is still developing, still deepening and still evolving over time. The values which underpin a great ethos won't change. How that ethos lives out those values may, however, shift over time.

Throw out the plan

One of the joys (and frustrations) of working with people is that nothing ever entirely goes to plan. You can map out what you want to happen. You can put together the actions that should get you to your destination, but then something unexpected happens. It always does. Even the unexpected should be seen as an opportunity though. It's an opportunity to demonstrate the values which are so important and underpin everything. It's an opportunity to show the care and compassion you have for others in navigating whatever the unexpected is with them. It's a chance to develop resilience and adaptability too. There are times when sticking to the plan is the right thing. When that forward planning and structure will see you through. There are, however, times when tearing the plan up and living out your values can be the right thing too. It's often a judgement call. It gets easier with time, but none of us gets it right every time. Taking that chance, living by your values, explaining that process and then accepting that we don't always get everything right and owning that can be valuable lessons for others to see. They demonstrate our credibility, our vulnerability and our humanity. When dealing with people, that can be really important.

So how do we develop ethos and values in the classroom?

Being clear on your own values is absolutely central. Everything flows from this.

Making sure everyone is included (and knows they are valued) is a beginning.

Ensuring that our actions are consistent with our values and understanding that often it's the small things that will be noticed is also an important step.

Finally, we need to have a plan, yet be adaptable and confident to react when needed.

The most important step is being really clear on your values. What do you hold dear? Why?

With a vast amount of experience, Oliver was someone I wanted to have heard in this book. To be able to have him start things off in this compendium of insights and ideas is fantastic. As you continue through this volume, you will find great practice backed by evidence, but if you want to be successful in the classroom, then it is vital that you understand who you are as a teacher and what motivates you. Identify that and when things get tough you will find yourself supported (propped up at times by those values and beliefs).

Understanding who you are as a teacher will help you thrive at specific schools as well. Very often, educators may be struggling; however, it is not the profession itself but the context they are in.

Currently, as a moderator of an edu-Facebook group with almost 30,000 followers, you hear about all sorts of practices and settings with vastly different ideologies. Before we place ourselves in a setting that we may not feel right in, taking the time to discover our ethos before we apply for these places is valuable. I think Oliver's thoughts on this are like gold dust and whether you are new in the profession or have more years under your belt, reflecting and reviewing on where you are is always a worthwhile exercise.

Reflecting on the voices of primary education

■ Put your beliefs about education into a few sentences.

_____

_____

_____

_____

■ Identify some key values that arise from these sentences.

_____

_____

_____

_____

■ How can you implement these values into your classroom or your school?

_____

_____

_____

_____

Building with a carrot and a stick

Matt Roberts

Ideas transcribed from Primary Education Voices Episode and blog with Chris Dyson

Chris Dyson is one of the most energetic and inspiring individuals I have met on the #edutwitter space. When I interviewed him on Primary Education Voices, I was blown away with his enthusiasm and love for ... well everything. Looking the part in his trademark waistcoat, Chris proceeded to give a blow-by-blow account of the journey that his school Parklands Primary in Leeds has been on. From padded cells and children on the roof to the place of love and inclusion it is now, the transformation has been remarkable. As such, I was eager to have his voice as part of the plethora of excellent educators you will hear from in this volume. Chris really did want to be included but with being in the process of creating his own book (Parklands: A School Built on Love) and running a very busy school as his day job, he wasn't able to pen it himself.

However, he has given me verbal permission to use the interview captured on Primary Education Voices, as well as his blog pinned on his Twitter profile ("This is what teachers need: Smiles and Love") to create an entry to include with the host of inspiring educators in this book. I was very pleased to accept his generous offer.

An ethos that works ...

To use Chris Dyson's own words:

> If teachers are treated as the brilliant individuals and life chang-ers that they are, success can be achieved without having to be a dictator – it can be achieved through smiles and love.

This is very much a message that he shared throughout his Primary Education Voices interview and one that underpins his school's ethos. When he arrived at Parklands Primary in Leeds, the school boasted a padded cell that children would be sent to for exclusions from the classroom. There were numerous children on the roof playing "tig," the school two years previously had been through five headteachers and enacted 150 exclusions. All of which painted a dreary picture where compassion and empathy were at an all-time low.

Now, after Chris' influential leadership, the school is a completely different space. Gone is the padded cell, staff retention is extremely high and the children are becoming proud of their achievements, being recognised on a national level. However, the understandable question is *how*? How in such a short space of time has this change been implemented.

It all comes down to the ethos that Chris has set in his school. He will be the first (and indeed he said this in his interview) to say that his approach or ethos is not necessarily the "way" that every school should be run or that he has unlocked the magic formula for school improvement. What is clear though is that when Chris began his journey at Parklands, he had a clear vision and ethos in mind.

Consistency with carrots, shunning the stick

For Chris, it was evident that in order to shift the attitude of the school, an approach that involved the staff, children and parents at the school was vital. From there, he sought to take them all on the journey with him.

Staff

In our interview, Chris shared how in the early stages of his leadership he was at first met with rolling eyes and glazed looks when he shared his aspirations for the school. After half a dozen headteachers within the space of a couple of years promising fresh starts, this was unsurprising. However, from that moment, it became clear that the key to gaining the buy-in from staff was to be consistency.

In primary education, we are busy with many tasks and things to complete but in order to build a vibrant, engaging school community Chris wanted to do more – reach out more. And so, he planned and implemented huge events in collaboration with local businesses. On Christmas Eve, Parklands provided Christmas lunches, a grotto and a disco as only 10 of his 304 children had ever had that experience before. Staff from the school pitched in to this ... but how?

From the beginning, Chris has made it clear that his staff are able to ask for flexibility in their work. If they are doing tasks that don't require them to be in front of the children or in school, then they can do it from home. If their own child has a sports day, they have family from a long way away visiting and so on – school provides a way for them to be able to attend those important events that may have had to be missed. Staff at Parklands feel incredibly valued as they are shown the trust to engage in these activities but not let the quality of learning drop for the children at the school.

From our discussion, it was clear that Chris attributes all the success that the school has had to his staff. They bought into his message because he talked a brilliant talk but backed it up with the walk that it required. To build a powerful ethos in a class or a school, then it takes consistency and valuing each member of that team (be it staff, children or parents) when they engage fully in that process.

Children

Of course, the staff may have been inspired to follow Chris on this journey. However, without the buy-in from the children, then it would not have had the same impact that has taken place at the school. For Chris, the approach he took with his staff was in a similar fashion with the children.

When he began his headship at Parklands, he told the children that they would have the best year they have ever had at the school. It would be very easy then to commence the school year, focus on school improvement and raise standards but again, as mentioned previously, he aimed to give the children truly unforgettable experiences.

Helicopters on the school field, thousands of pounds raised to sponsor residentials, whole school visits to the beach and every child with a Cornetto … the list could go on with the memorable events that these children have been given since the ethos of the carrot began at Parklands. As always, backing up your ethos with action being pivotal.

However, what struck me in Chris' explanations of what his school has done was not necessarily the grand events, but what he mentioned about how his school work with the children in the classroom. He was very explicit about how whenever there is a problem that his staff are trained to listen with love and seek to understand where the children are at. Previously, there were very strict sanctions for all manner of things, including the types of socks the children wore in an attempt to get them all in line.

The ethos at Parklands is far different now. It is a focus on the child, their emotions and seeking to understand their actions – why they may have struck out – and helping them to understand other ways to react. Once the staff team were led from the front with this inclusive, empathetic ethos, they were able to take this on board and make great impact in how they carry this out with the children.

Parents

When considering how to embed the ethos into a school setting, parents are often overlooked. Perhaps it is because we are focused on what happens day-to-day within the walls of the school itself. However, they are vital stakeholders that need to be brought on board as well from the very beginning. Again, this is applicable if you lead a school or a class. Starting off on the right foot with all the parents you can is a sure-fire way to improve outcomes in your class or school. The EEF (2022) published an evidence review that highlighted the importance of positive parental engagement. They found that sending personalised texts or letters to parents can improve attendance. Taking this evidence on board, improved attendance will lead to better outcomes. As such, bringing parents on board to the ethos of your class or school is a required step.

Chris understood this incredibly when his journey began at Parklands. He had a completely open-door policy, making it clear that parents could speak to him so that the teachers could get on with the business of teaching. Of course, teachers were available, but if there was a problem, then he was there to address it. This is different from numerous settings where the policy is to speak to the class teacher first, then a member of SLT, then the Deputy Head and then finally, after a couple of weeks, the Head. Yet, Chris wanted to show the parents of his school the dedication he had to their voices.

In his first meeting with parents at Parklands (after bringing in doughnuts from Marks and Spencers), only three people came – with two not even having children at the school! It would have been very easy for him to bemoan the lack of engagement, put the blame on the supposed apathy from parents, perhaps the area his school was in. However, he reached out on the playground. He spoke personally with every parent he could and did it again the week after … and the week after … until eventually there were about 80 parents that came to listen to his vision. Now, after years of personal outreach and an ethos of inviting the parents, Parklands regularly has 200 parents visiting for a FunDay Friday Celebration Assembly.

What was the key message from this incredible success?

Again, the message rings clear throughout all of Chris' work. Consistency, dedication and backing up the outstanding talk with equally powerful action. Too often we seem to have a divide between school and parents, an attitude that parents are either not engaged enough or too demanding. The reality is that each parent wants what is best for their child and they just maybe haven't caught the ethos or vision of your class or school. If they haven't, then it is down to you as the teacher or leader to communicate that in some way. Whatever method you can use that suits your context is brilliant, but when we humanise schools and help parents (who are sometimes intimidated by educational settings) see that we are open, loving and embracing (if that is your context), then they will support you far more. Chris has demonstrated this at Parklands.

Lessons from building a school with love

So, above are some key takeaways from materials that Chris has given me permission to use in this collection of excellent primary practitioners. The question is what can we glean from it – after all, we are not all like Chris Dyson. Honestly, I don't think anyone is! However, there are some important messages we can take about establishing a clear ethos in a classroom or a school.

1. Be clear yourself what your vision is – Chris knew what he wanted to focus on and develop as the atmosphere of his school.
2. Communicate this ethos clearly with your staff – of course, you may want to involve your staff or children in developing what the ethos looks like but once it's finalised, do this with clarity. It could be on moving up days with a new class, informally meeting parents on the playground – anywhere! Share it! Live it!
3. Be consistent in modelling the ethos – this is the hardest message to implement. It means even on those miserable, dark mornings in January, rain pelting down on you as you enter the building when you've had a late night trying to complete a certain task or sorting a family commitment. You then have to live the ethos you want to set in the class or school.

I'm sure there are many more things we learn from Chris and his thoughts but one thing is for sure. Setting an ethos or attitude for your class or for your school is the very first step you must take before then embarking on developing the practice that will then take your school to the next level!

Reflecting on the voices of primary education

■ If you were to summarise Chris Dyson's ethos – what would it be?

_____

_____

_____

_____

_____

_____

■ What key messages did you notice about how the ethos at Parklands Primary was developed?

_____

_____

_____

_____

_____

_____

■ What would you like to try and work on to embed the ethos you desire in your class or school?

_____

_____

_____

_____

_____

_____

References

Dyson, C. This is what teachers need: Smiles and Love. https://www.integritycoaching. co.uk/blog/what-teachers-need

EEF (2022). New: Evidence review finds sending personalised letters or texts can help but wider evidence is weak. https://educationendowmentfoundation. org.uk/news/new-evidence-review-finds-sending-personalised-letters-or-texts-can-help-but-wider-evidence-is-weak

2

Relationships in education

Penny Whelan – @pennywpennyw
Victoria Carr – @HappyHead74
Clare Campbell – @ClareCampbell7

If the atmosphere and ethos you build in the classroom was collectively the first most often thing said in our Primary Education Voices chats, then the relationships we build with the class were the second most often said thing. The relationships we develop with the class are of course of vital importance as are the links we create with fellow staff members, colleagues across different settings and so on. These working relationships can shift the paradigm that we use in our classroom as we build understanding with each other.

In this chapter, we will first hear from Penny Whelan who gives an excellent overview of key individuals we need to build stronger relationships with: staff, children and other settings. Flowing on neatly we will learn from Dr Vic Carr who will reinforce the need for collaboration to improve our settings. We conclude with some thoughts that I have developed alongside Dr Clare Campbell. She gives some valuable insights into this theme and will share how the relationships we build with the children we teach can develop a stronger sense of self-esteem for them.

Building and developing relationships in education

Penny Whelan

Healthy working relationships in teaching are pivotal to getting the very best from yourself and those around you. Everyone needs support and anyone who says they don't isn't being

DOI: 10.4324/9781003307150-2

truthful, and certainly isn't prepared for the reality of life as a teacher. It's a journey where you are constantly learning and developing, observing others, stealing ideas and questioning your practice – and it's this that makes you stronger! You learn from those around you and they learn from you, and it's a cycle that keeps us strong, united and supportive of each other.

Building relationships in school – With staff

Your colleagues are your work family, and a good working relationship with them is an essential tool to finding happiness in the workplace. People go about building these relationships in different ways, and how you choose to do it is up to you. Are you the kind of person who tells people about yourself, what your family is like, what hobbies you have, etc.? Or are you more of a private person who likes to keep work and home separate? Either way, there are things you can do to create good working relationships that will reflect who you are and your core values, whilst also adding to the ethos and culture of the school.

1. Be a good listener – Be an active listener and make sure you really pay attention when people are speaking to you. If you make time for others, they'll make time for you and that is invaluable, especially when you've had a tough day (spoiler – you will have tough days!) or when you've got a question you need to ask. We all know how to project the right body language, but something that has always stuck with me is this .... Never glance at your phone or your watch whilst speaking to someone. If you need to check the time, do it when you are the one who's talking and not someone else. If you do it whilst they are speaking, they'll think you're not interested. Never underestimate the importance of listening to people. You can have a huge impact by simply giving someone your time and attention.
2. Take an interest in others – We all need people to take an interest in us. It makes us feel valued and increases our sense of self-worth and belonging. Ask people how they are when they have been ill, tell them you missed them in school, ask what they are up to at the weekend, etc. Don't just exist alongside your colleagues, but be a positive influence on each other's lives. Not everyone wants to

share what they do every day with the people they work with, but it's important to check in on each other. Teaching is amazing but it's incredibly exhausting and intense, and someone asking if you are ok can really mean the world. You might just pick up on something that someone really needs help with. It's the difference between leaving work smiling or leaving crying after a difficult day. It's the difference between talking about our emotions and our mental health and hiding it. It's the difference between isolation and inclusion. Community is everything.

3. Be open and honest – Again, that doesn't mean you have to share everything you do with the people you work with, but it does mean showing them that you are vulnerable sometimes, that you make mistakes and you're not afraid to admit them. Always apologise if you know you need to and make things right. We will always have disagreements with others but it's not that which is the problem, it's how we choose to resolve it and move on. A leader who can show their colleagues that they make mistakes or that they feel down and struggle sometimes, will be a stronger leader with a team willing to follow them. You're not invincible, and you don't have to pretend you are either.

4. Be kind – As my friend John Magee would say, Kindness matters! It's something that is underrated in my opinion but something so important. Showing kindness to colleagues is probably the simplest way to build and retain meaningful relationships, and it can stem from the smallest gestures.

So what are the benefits of teaching and learning? How will positive relationships with colleagues improve your practice? You'll feel more confident and comfortable around your colleagues and they around you and it paves the way for collaborative learning and working. People will feel valued and heard and you will be able to work together much more efficiently.
Why not ...?

■ Share resources with people to help decrease the workload – why reinvent the wheel? If you have something that might help someone else, or you know a good website that would do the job, pass it on! Hopefully, they'll do the same for you too.

- Observe as many other teachers as you can and invite them to observe you – it helps you get used to having people in your classroom and increases confidence. It also helps to share ideas and get feedback from people who know you well.
- Ask if you can observe colleagues in other schools and visit other settings – it's great to be able to get out and see what other people across the town and country are doing. You'll pick up lots of ideas and hopefully build relationships with people outside of your organisation too.
- Create a CPD library in the staffroom that all staff can access and invite them to contribute to it – help each other to learn by sharing research, articles and books.
- Work with colleagues to lead staff meetings and CPD sessions – or do them on your own of course! Leading training can be scary and tough, but if you've got a good rapport and build trust with your colleagues, they'll support you and be a fantastic audience.

Being a teacher can feel lonely at times, in your own classroom with the door closed, just 30 children and you, but you're strongest when you work with others and support each other.

Building relationships in school – With pupils

We've all heard the "don't smile until half term" saying that's always told to new teachers, but actually, if your children fear you and don't trust you, will they really be comfortable and confident in your class? It might sound like common sense, but if you build a strong relationship based on mutual respect with the children in your class, the atmosphere will ultimately be more conducive to learning. Happy, comfortable children that feel valued and included will give you far more of their attention and stand more chance of going on to be confident and keen learners in the future.

1. Teach respect and kindness – If the children I have taught over the years remember only to "be kind" to others (obviously, I hope there will be more that they retain from my

teaching though – fingers crossed), then I'll consider it a job well done. The world needs kindness, and the best way to teach this is to be the role model ourselves. Be kind to the pupils and teach them to care about the world they live in and about each other but show them how to do it.

2. Give them your time – make sure you spend time with each child in your class as much as you can, not just over their work, but first thing in the morning or at break time when they want to chat. Often a child has come to tell me something about their weekend, and it's usually whilst I'm rushing off to a meeting or trying to balance a huge pile of books as I walk to the staffroom, but I always try and make time to listen to them. Stop what you're doing and really listen for a few minutes, or if you can't at that time, ask them to come back to you later on because you're really interested in what they want to share. After all, a child who feels heard when they want to tell you about their new kitten or Gran's visit from abroad is far more likely to trust you and share their difficulties and concerns, and we don't want them to hide things that upset them.

3. Trust them – Give them jobs and responsibilities that they can be proud of and that will show you that you trust them. There are so many things in your classroom that the children can help take responsibility for and they will love to help you and show you they can do it. Make sure you give everyone a chance to take on some of those roles and don't always choose the same children or the ones that you think are capable. Everyone is capable if you show them what to do and support them. Show them how to trust.

4. Be inclusive – This is a hugely important one and covers so much. Inclusion means making everyone feel accepted, part of the class and valued. It covers children with special educational needs and/or disabilities (and as a SENCO, I'm passionate about this one), children with English as an additional language, children with different behaviours or personal needs and so much more. Make sure that every single child in your class feels like part of the community. Make sure that what you teach, what you show and the resources you share are inclusive and representative of that same class community. Diversity, inclusion and equality should always be evident in your

classroom. It is important to remember, however, that equality doesn't always mean giving everyone access to the same support. Different needs require different support systems; thus, Equity is also an important factor.

So, again, what are the benefits of teaching and learning? How will positive relationships with the children in your class improve your practice? I've answered a lot of this in the points above, but it really is this simple .... If you have fostered and nurtured a good positive relationship with your students, you will get the best from each other. They will feel included, valued and respected, and that is the best environment for growth and learning.

Building relationships between schools (for staff and students)

Since 2009, my Local Authority has been part of The Linking Network, a charity based in Bradford that helps to make and support meaningful links between pairs of schools. The children in one school learn about and meet pupils from another, usually from the same town or county, who might not normally come across each other in day-to-day life. The basic principles are rooted in exploring identity, promoting diversity, celebrating community and developing equality, and schools arrange a series of meetings between pupils from each school so that they can get to know each other and explore different topics in a fun environment. It's all about building relationships with new people.

There are lots of ways to allow teachers to forge connections with other schools, but I have found that The Linking Network is particularly effective at bringing people together in the simplest way. By working with a colleague from another school and arranging for your two classes to meet, you inadvertently build a relationship with your partner teacher and become the role model for the pupils. You can then choose how to continue that connection and it's fantastic to have professional links with other people in your locality.

However great it is for the teachers, the benefits from "Linking" for the pupils are enormous in comparison. Our young people learn to work well with others they see daily and sit next to in lessons, even those they attend clubs with after school or at the weekend, but how many of them have the opportunity to meet new people from different areas, backgrounds, cultures or religions? This is what The Linking Network can provide for schools and pupils. It's a chance to ask questions in a safe environment, to meet new people, to learn alongside others and to realise that we are part of a global community. It's well-structured and planned, making it easy for teachers to deliver. They learn about the similarities and differences that we share and those things which make us special and unique. They learn to think about global issues and are given the chance to make a real change in their community by taking part in a social action project.

The children that learn to build relationships with those outside of their own school are the ones that will be best equipped to go on to secondary school, will appreciate the diverse world in which we live and will grow to be kind, tolerant, accepting and respectful of different needs, cultures and religions.

It's all about relationships.

One thing that became clear as I interviewed dozens of inspirational Primary colleagues is that there was often one particular thing that stood out as key to developing children in primary schools in every area – academic, social, emotional and so on. It was relationships.

The relationships we have with the children and staff in the school are the lifeblood of the atmosphere and environment we seek to establish in our institutions. What makes your school what it is? Is it the buildings, the curriculum or the location? I would hazard a guess that it is the people – staff and children – that truly define your school and the relationships they have with each other.

That's why I wanted Penny to contribute to this book as she shared some excellent practice in this area, including the work with The Linking Network which was something that I had never come across before. What an incredible way to break down boundaries, foster tolerance and create understanding within our children for others who come from different contexts and backgrounds. I'm sure that we can all take some time to reflect and consider how we can build stronger relationships with all those we come into contact with in our day-to-day school interactions.

Reflecting on the voices of primary education

■ What is something you are going to do to develop relationships further with staff in your school?

_____

_____

_____

_____

_____

■ What is something you are going to do to develop relationships further with children in your school?

_____

_____

_____

_____

_____

■ What is something you are going to do to develop relationships with staff and children in other schools?

_____

_____

_____

_____

_____

Collaboration. Collaboration. Collaboration.

Dr Victoria Carr

Teaching can feel like a very lonely space at times, as can leadership.

I would be surprised to find an educational practitioner who advocates for solo working, who doesn't appreciate the value and enrichment of collaboration with others – after all, don't we all agree with the old adage that "two minds are better than one"?

Anecdotally, we all know the emotional and psychological benefits associated with working closely with colleagues in high-functioning and supportive teams when planning, discussing and problem-solving. The COVID-19 pandemic and the measures we all had to work under for prolonged periods merely highlighted many of the things that we all accepted. We know, for example, that in working collaboratively feelings of isolation can be mitigated, a holistic sense of wellbeing can be fostered, the opportunity for burnout can be reduced, as can the likelihood of colleagues competing in a toxic way with one another.

Yet, as a teacher, unless you have a child in your class who needs support in the form of another adult, whole days can go by without conversation with anyone other than the pupils in your class. Whilst this can be heart-warming, because we love our children and enjoy their observations on life, there are times when talking through an idea, an issue or an opportunity with a colleague can make a significant difference. Yet the way our contemporary education system is configured leaves little to no time for this kind of developmental activity.

We know there are myriad reasons for this phenomenon including but not limited to the following: accountability measures which can mean that every second of time is focused on pupils learning (to pass tests); the lost learning/lost-generation narrative which can mean that there is ever more pressure on learning time, and this can even involve before and after school catch up sessions; competing priorities in the school day and the increase in curriculum expectation which can mean that just ensuring curricular provision squeezes out all opportunities for conversation with other practitioners; and finally, as if all of that isn't enough, the pandemic response we have all adhered to means that we have not even been able to have a cup of tea or lunch with our colleagues in a staff room for informal conversations (assuming calling parents, emailing professionals, updating SEND/pastoral information on systems such as C-POMS has all been completed).

I work on the hypothesis that collaboration among educational practitioners could be a transformational force that positively influences not just the school, but the whole community. I believe that anyone in a position to influence lives, such as those working in schools, should take this responsibility seriously and see themselves as role models at all times for colleagues, parents and children, both in their own setting and beyond. Whilst this means that you have to set and maintain the highest standards, and live by your values, the impact can ripple across generations and is therefore well worth the effort required.

I believe that role modelling in education encapsulates more than just how we enact our relationships with one another, the language we use to and about ourselves and others, how we behave in contested situations and how we build resilience and respect. I think that it is important in a learning community for adults to model learning, how it is done, the barriers we face to successfully being able to learn, how we overcome them, what motivates us and how learning can enhance our knowledge, understanding, lives, job prospects and opportunities that present themselves. Part of that body of understanding in a community of practice is achieved through openly sharing systems, processes, strategies for planning, teaching, pupil and adult-centred growth, to bring about professional development for colleagues and to elicit key learning points from any mistakes made as well as successes.

In order to create a high-functioning thriving collaborative learning community, the vast majority of staff have to buy in to this model, in all its many guises, and its potential outcomes, and in my experience this is usually an organic process, based on seeing colleagues doing it and discussing how they can follow suit – in other words, by coaching.

Whilst I have no definitive empirical evidence to support my view, nor do I have any to contest it. Thus I advocate for a

collaborative professional learning community in which effi-
cacious and forward-thinking and progressive practitioners
share, challenge and develop the expertise of one another,
and I have spent considerable time crafting such a community in the schools I have been privileged enough to lead.

It is commonly accepted that educators can play a crucial role in co-creating the happiness, academic performance, and thus attainment of their students, sometimes
even being able to override the home lives of those who are
the most vulnerable in our society and who have significant
social, emotional and behavioural needs (I am living proof
of this). We, as leaders, are tasked with ensuring that the
capacity of our staff to invest in pupils in a healthy and productive way is paramount and the mental health of our staff
is therefore rightly given prominence in much rhetoric by the
Department for Education, yet we are financially hamstrung
and given limited resources to enable this without considerable creativity.

We know that in order to feel empowered, skilled and able,
staff need continuous professional development in terms of
not just teaching strategy and pedagogy to ensure cohesion
and progression in lessons but also in coaching, mentoring and supervision. We know that if we want to keep well
trained and highly competent practitioners in our schools,
then they need to be incentivised and feel a sense of job
satisfaction alongside the inherent fulfilment that comes with
working with children and young people. The truth is, leaders
are constantly debating how this can be achieved with dimin-
ished or non-existent budgets, limited time during the school
day, limited opportunities for face-to-face meetings, fewer
staff in smaller schools and a cornucopia of other issues?

Within your own school, as a Headteacher, you are able
to choose the culture that you want to create. If you choose
to do professional or academic study outside of school,
then it is possible to normalise this as an activity and it
is possible to demonstrate how you find the time around
family and social life, and with the backdrop of constraints
around workload for other colleagues. It is possible to fund
or part fund courses and development as part of a suite of
professional opportunities you create for staff. If you want
to support staff in planning, then it is possible to create

opportunity for collaborative Planning Preparation and Assessment (PPA) time across year groups (if you are more than 1 form entry) or phases (if you are 1 form or less). It is possible to minimise bureaucracy and administrative tasks that staff have to complete to those that are essential in order to facilitate effective teaching by reviewing policy and practice in areas such as marking and assessment. BUT, and there is a but, for every decision that you take to create this "weather" and culture in your school, another decision must be made on what you want to let go of. The competing priorities of any educational setting mean that at any time leaders are balancing need and want, ideal and manageable, essential and desirable, affordable and necessary. For me, this is a constant challenge but I am resolute that working as a team is the way that I want to work – for us it is successful, and I am aware that I am lucky (in a 3-form entry school) to have the capacity to work in a collaborative way as I have enough human resource and diversity in skill set to make this work.

This can be, in itself, a complicated task given the inconsistencies and nuances of understanding teacher collaboration, whether this is superficial or profound and whether it is tokenistic or authentic. I feel that our model, in its maturity, now offers more of the profound and authentic than when the school was in crisis and we had significant systemic change to make. The absence of a unified theory, or seminal research, on the positive or negative effects of teacher collaboration, as well as a consistent definition of the concept, can lead to mixed and inconsistent results within schools which could make the evaluation of effectiveness of collaboration as an approach very difficult. This is compounded when you try to collaborate across other schools, something that is essential for smaller schools as they simply do not have the human resources.

Positive impacts of the growth of social media platforms during the last 10 years and their use in education forums are that collaboration across all phases and sectors from Pupil Referral Units (PRUs) to special schools, nurseries to universities is now commonplace and support available day and night for those with a vested interest in the global, as well as national education debates of our times. This is something that I actively exploit in school, as do my staff by extension. As a result, we are part of several different and equally rewarding professional collaborative groups that have provided an emotional, practical, professional and academic handrail to many members of my school community – particularly during the pandemic.

Schools collaborate throughout the year, for a multitude of reasons, with varying degrees of success in terms of purpose, impact and sustainability; however, very little research exists to support or challenge the reasons why. The inter-school dynamic encompasses a wide range of different activities on both a formal and informal basis and with the advent of Multi Academy Trusts (MATs) a hybrid of both, involving schools of different phases. It is a truism that despite the measurable increase in the level of inter-school collaborative activity, particularly over the last decade through the academisation agenda, the academic knowledge base in this area remains limited. The fact that schools compete for pupils, popularity with parents via Ofsted inspections and as a result of league tables, and funding which is directly related to numbers of pupils (and those who have specific needs) means that true "collaboration" can be problematic, and this really hinders the ability and drive to actually devote time and resources to facilitating collaboration across schools.

This means that the landscape of inter-school collaboration is more complex than ever and continues to be fundamentally affected, as it has in the last 40 years, by ever-increasing accountability and performativity in the neoliberal construct of education that has been fostered. It is highly likely that this agenda will be at the forefront of education as we navigate the 2020s and beyond and therefore the wisest of school leaders horizon scanning for both opportunity and threat at all times will be invested in collaborating as much as possible to ensure operational integrity in both the shorter and longer term.

One cannot read Vic's comments and not feel enthused to get out there find ways to make connections and relationships with other settings and excellent individuals. It is not surprising that the educational landscape has changed drastically over the last decade and this seems to have been coincided with the explosion of professional discussions on platforms like Twitter and sharing best practice over long distances.

As Vic outlines, up-to-date evidence on the impact of school's developing working relationships with each other on their own students' outcomes is limited. However, as we have heard from our other contributors in this chapter, building strong relationships in the classroom is key to effective teaching and learning. As such, might we suppose that this extends to the learning and development of our staff when we build such connections with other enthusiastic, like-minded professionals? Not to mention how we can share great practice and insights with each other.

Reflecting on the voices of primary education

■ What networks are you currently involved in that influence your practice?

_____

_____

_____

_____

_____

_____

■ Which areas of your teaching, learning or school would ben-efit from connecting with a network, group or individuals to develop yourself?

_____

_____

_____

_____

_____

_____

■ Are there any areas of your practice that you feel you could develop with the input of other professionals with an understanding of research and experience in that area?

_____

_____

_____

_____

_____

_____

Self-esteem is at the heart of education

Dr Clare Campbell

Dr Clare Campbell is an advocate for children's well-being, having published numerous publications focused on developing a well-rounded child and supporting them to have a healthier outlook on life. It is no surprise that for her, developing nurturing and powerful relationships is an integral part of Primary Education. Perhaps this was born in the example of her family who were also employed in Primary Education:

My Auntie Dot who helped to raise me was a Deputy Head at a Primary School and she was always my inspiration. She loved books and storytelling, drawing and painting, and she has passed all those loves on to me. I have always wanted to be a teacher for as long as I can remember. I used to line my dolls and teddies up the stairs and teach them from an easel in my hallway. It was my favourite game. I have always loved working with young children, it is such a privilege to be part of their childhoods as their teacher and headteacher.

As Primary educators we have a direct role in developing the next generation and when you consider which adults had the most influence on you in your development, it is those who spent the time to create real relationships – not the most intelligent or not even necessarily the most effective teachers. Whilst this is something that cannot be bottled or developed the same way with every child, it is something that we can seek to recognise more in Primary Education – particularly as we are often the first places that children go to for long periods of time without the company of their parents.

"Our identity is the difference about us that makes a difference. It must always be grounded in a social context—in a relationship" (Bradshaw, 1996).

Developing strong relationships with the children that we teach can have the most impact on teaching and learning in the classroom. There are a number of factors for this but Dr Campbell cites one of these as the capacity to develop a child's self-esteem:

Self-esteem is the key to learning. I wrote this in my very first essay as a primary teaching student aged over 23 years, and I still believe that it is true today. If a child has low self-esteem, then they are not in a good place to take on board any new learning. So much of a teacher's job is about their relationships with their pupils and the pastoral care of them. Children's mental health and well-being is of paramount importance, now more than ever and we should do everything in our power to build up a child's self-esteem. It can be a very fragile thing. That is why I love the creative subjects so much. Art, Drama, Dance, Music, Creative writing and poetry are areas of the curriculum where there are no wrong answers and where children can express themselves without fear of getting it wrong.

In my school, we use art therapy for our children who need additional support. We employ an art psychotherapist part-time to work with our children. Art therapy is about the process of art-making and building positive relationships with the therapist. The end product is not as important, but often our children do discover natural talent and go on to pursue art as a hobby, which can give them great joy and raise their self-esteem when they see that they are developing skills and unlocking their creative potential.

Those of you who are regular listeners to the podcast will know about my … tenuous relationship with art. As I look back, however, I think I begin to realise what went wrong and Dr Campbell's insights have helped me to reflect on this ….

I used to love Art in primary school. The opportunity to express myself and create was something that I enjoyed to the point that there was even a period of time at home that I chose to create pieces of art, working on these in my spare time as it gave me the headspace to find periods of calm. Looking back on my pieces of art they were not ... fantastic but I was always praised by my teachers, had positive elements highlighted and given steps to improve which I relished.

Then, I transitioned to secondary school. My art teacher was not unkind or cruel, but there was a method in her grading which destroyed my interest in art or anything creative. With each piece of homework, we were set and assigned a number and a letter. The number indicated how "good" the piece of art was. I seem to remember once reaching the lofty heights of a "7" but my average would have been around the 4/5 mark.

However, the letter was the rancour of my enthusiasm. We were assigned a letter between a-e, "a" meaning we had put the most amount of effort in, "e" meaning we had not put enough effort at all in our art pieces. I slaved (and I don't use that word lightly) for hours each week, determined to at least show I had put the effort in. Yet each week I would rarely be graded above a "c" ....

As such, I have spent years, over a decade, with a dislike for anything artistic, worried that people may judge what I create (and they still sometimes do). However, Dr Campbell's approach of building strong relationships through the arts strikes me as a strong way to improve a child's view of themselves and that will have untold effects on their learning and development.

Ensuring that a child's or young person's strengths and protective factors are realised to their full potential is likely to help to improve outcomes by building their protective network (Daniel and Wassell 2002).

Dr Campbell further invites us to reflect on any intentional or unintentional ceilings we place over a child's development:

Never underestimate a child. I think one of the most dangerous things we can do as educators is to underestimate a child. To have low expectations of them, to put a ceiling on their natural gifts and talents is wrong. That is why I am not a big fan of a data-driven school. Children are so much more than a SATs score or a grade on their phonics screening test.

I have seen children work creatively together to produce some incredible things.

During the lockdown, our Head Girl Emily was diagnosed with leukaemia and she has undergone a punishing treatment schedule of chemotherapy during her time in Years 5 and 6. That little girl was completing schoolwork to the highest standards while in her hospital bed. Her family, her friends and our school managed to raise over £4500 during the pandemic for children in Manchester Children's Hospital. Her classmates went on sponsored bike rides, shaved their hair and made little bead angels to sell. They created beautiful artwork for her and got celebrities all over the country engaged in a Thumbs Up for Emily campaign on social media. Her favourite rugby player, Jackson Hastings, wore special rugby boots dedicated to her in a rugby match. She has done things I never expected or dreamed she could do. But I never underestimated her strength, her will and her determination. We have all got a lot to learn from our children about dignity, integrity, compassion and kindness. She is my hero.

How can we possibly expect children to reach the highest standards that they can reach if we predetermine their journey? We must develop strong relationships with the children that we teach in order to better understand how much they can challenge and push themselves. Setting learning opportunities without understanding each child means they have no agency to act for themselves in their learning and therefore can feel demotivated to put forward their best efforts.

Improved teacher self-efficacy can result in improved teacher mental health and job satisfaction, and students' academic performance (Bandura, 1977).

Finally, Clare develops our understanding of building relationships and how these unlock the door for learning by explaining that we must be ourselves. Often, we may see the "outstanding" teachers in our school and seek to replicate their methods. However, those who have tried this may experience some discomfort. That is because they are not you – you must teach the way you are. Whilst this can be difficult to quantify or explain, Clare shares the potential power of being ourselves in all of this:

Be Yourself. Over the years, I have worked in three different primary schools, in lots of different roles, class teacher,

SENDCo, Art Lead, RE lead, English Lead, Assistant Head, Headteacher, RE Inspector and Lecturer in HE. In every role and in each school, I have always tried to stay true to myself. I am not a dragon, I don't shout at children or humiliate them, or make examples of them and when I started in headship, some of the staff were expecting that. Some of them thought that that was how a headteacher should behave. They thought it was good if children were frightened of them. That is just not me and it never will be. Sometimes I have tried new things and I have received criticism from parents or staff about introducing new methods, but if I can hand on heart say that all the decisions I have made have had the children's best interests at heart, then I have done my job. I have to be a champion for the children. I have to make decisions that put the needs of the children first and sometimes the needs of the most vulnerable children first, not the needs of the staff, the parents or the governors. I have to stay true to myself, my core values of compassion, service, kindness and love, I genuinely love my job. I love learning and I know I will continue learning for the rest of my life. It is this passion for learning that I want to pass on to the children in my care every day. Be yourself, at interview, in the classroom, in front of staff, in front of parents, and most importantly in front of the children every day. Be true to yourself.

These comments from Clare just make me wonder what a joy it would be to teach and learn in her school! Relationships are clearly at the core of her leadership and the way she desires her teachers to teach. When considering what the best thing about being in Primary Education, this is abundantly clear:

The children are the best thing about being in Primary Education of course! You can't help but smile when you go and chat to them. If ever I'm having a difficult day, I go and spend time with some of our youngest children, who in my school are only 3. They are so full of fun, they see the awe and wonder in the tiniest things and they are often in fits of helpless giggles, which is adorable and infectious. We have a school sausage dog Charley who comes into school with me everyday and the children love her, she is also one of the very best things about my school.

Reflecting on the voices of primary education

- What specific things can you do in your practice to develop the self-esteem of the children that you teach?

_____

_____

_____

_____

_____

_____

- How can your practice give space for children to make more choices about their learning opportunities to avoid underestimating them?

_____

_____

_____

_____

_____

_____

- How would you describe your "style" of teaching and does it reflect your personality?

_____

_____

_____

_____

_____

_____

References

Bandura, A. (1977). Self-efficacy: Toward a unifying theory of behavioral change. Psychol. Rev. 84, 191–215. doi: 10.1037/0033-295X.84.2.191

Bradshaw, J. (1996). Bradshaw On: The Family. A New Way of Creating Solid Self-Esteem. Health Communications, Inc., Deerfield Beach, FL.

Daniel, B. and Wassell, S. (2002). Assessing and Promoting Resilience in Vulnerable Children. Jessica Kingsley, London.

3

Curriculum leadership and design

Matt Roberts – @Mroberts90Matt
Tom Griffiths – @TJGriffiths

Developing the wider curriculum is an area of Primary Education that has taken centre stage over the last five years or so. With the new Ofsted Frameworks in the late-2010s which shifted the focus to diving deeper into the whole curriculum (rather than just a focus on data from English and Maths), schools have taken measures to address what were the weaker areas of their curriculum. Such measures included appointing "Curriculum Leads," developing subject leaders and making their leadership development more of a priority and diving deeper into foundation subjects. As such, we have had a number of discussions on the Primary Education Voices podcast about developing this area, in particular looking at how to support subject leaders.

As I personally have a great passion for this area and seek to be a supportive influence to subject leaders that I work with, I have outlined some insights into how to develop leadership of the curriculum. These ideas may be useful for senior leaders who are looking to develop this area in their school as well as teachers who themselves are subject leaders or seek to become so. Tom Griffiths will then share his practice in this area and in particular how his school has used "Curriculum Coaches" to help this work on curriculum

DOI: 10.4324/9781003307150-3

move forward. The reality is that a school's curriculum will only be as strong as the leaders who carry the "expertise" of their subjects.

Ideas for curriculum leadership

Matt Roberts

My first foray into thinking deeply about curriculum development was when I had the opportunity to apply for an internal vacancy in my school as a Curriculum Lead. This was in 2017, the time when Ofsted began their consultation into directing more focus on the curriculum. It was a time when schools became familiar with the words "Intent," "Implementation" and "Impact," when knowledge organisers became vogue and when the term "deep dive" would be thrown around and cause shudders in any teacher that had been in the job for more than three years.

Looking back at the developments in the framework and the drive on improving standards in all aspects of the curriculum, not just the data-heavy English and Maths, I feel that this has been a positive change for primary education. Of course, I am not so sure about how Ofsted has carried out this framework, not to mention the madness of schools being directed to improve standards across a dozen different subjects with less funding and training. There is also something to say about the loss of funding and promotion around other areas of supporting teaching and learning because of this framework shift – such as teaching children who speak English as an Additional Language (Ofsted abolished the role of National Lead for EAL, ESOL and Gypsy, Roma and Travellers in 2021).

However, since my introduction to the role of the curriculum, it has become clear to me that the curriculum should be the lifeblood of an effective school.

Subject leaders – Key to an effective curriculum

One principle that I championed in that initial job application was the role of subject leaders. With 11 subjects to raise standards in across six-year groups – not to mention how English is often divided between two leads for Reading and Writing – you begin to see why one person cannot do this successfully. In fact, if you break down 12 subjects across six-year groups into six half terms (the usual amount of time allotted to a "unit" in a primary school), there is a total of 432 units taught in a primary school each year (not to mention when multiple concepts are covered in a half term such as in Maths and the entire EYFSP)! As such, well-trained subject leaders who are unified on the vision of the school's curriculum are a must for a curriculum that works.

The factors that make an effective subject leader are discussed in many publications and articles. Those of you reading will have different roles.

Senior Leaders: Your role is to empower and train these subject leaders to become leaders of their subject, rather than managers of their stock cupboard. The natural instinct we have as senior leaders is to pass the monitoring and evaluation of each subject to the subject leaders – give them time to look through books and gather pupil voice. However, if the subject leader hasn't been given time and direction to be able to formulate what best practice in their subject looks like, they will only look at surface-level aspects of their curriculum such as at how the books are looking.

You are in your position because some people felt that you had the skills and knowledge to lead effectively on school development. Some of your subject leaders may well have these skills too. Use them, give them the platform to lead and inspire other subject leaders and provide a template for others on how they can grow and nurture their subject.

Other subject leaders may not have these skills naturally, yet. Apply that growth mindset thinking we often apply to our classrooms and go about providing opportunities for them. They may need some scaffolding and support, and that's ok. There is a big difference between telling someone to go and be ready to answer big questions about their subject and letting them try and figure it out and providing prompting questions for them to consider.

For example, instead of just providing a big box labelled "Intent" and expecting a new or developing subject leader to fill in their vision for their subject, break it down for them:

INTENT	
What do you want your subject to look like at _____?	
How does it relate to the National Curriculum?	
How does your subject show progression across the school?	

Further to that, you may want to guide your subject leaders further by giving them specific aspects of their curriculum to reflect on, such as:

INTENT	
What do you want your subject to look like at ____? What are the ethos and values that underpin the teaching and learning in your subject? What role do knowledge and experiences play in your subject?	
How does it relate to the National Curriculum? What key points are drawn from the National Curriculum? What non-statutory points are covered in your subject alongside the statutory objectives?	
How does your subject show progression across the school? How do you as a subject leader evidence progression across the school in your subject? Why are the topics in your subject plotted the way they are from Y1 to Y6? Are teachers that teach your subject aware of the previous year's objectives and next year's objectives to support their planning? How are concepts developed across your curriculum such as "Democracy", "Trade" or "Sources"?	

As subject leaders, your role is to support and guide your leaders, not just leave them to figure it out on their own.

Let's talk about time. It is becoming more standard practice to provide some time to subject leaders to get to grips with their subjects. This is good. It needs to happen. A well-crafted curriculum cannot work unless the subject leaders are given time to seek out resources, training and materials to improve their subject. However, rather than giving generic time and expecting a focused output from that time, consider giving direction for this time.

For example, subject leaders could be asked to:

- Reflect on how your subject caters to our specific school community's diversity. Are all children in our school population represented at some stage in your subject? Use evidence from books, pupil voice and our intended curriculum to consider this.
- Are we able to provide a rationale for the sequence of content in your subject? Using the National Curriculum, our progression of skills/knowledge and evidence from pupil's learning, prepare to share responses with staff so they can explain why their content comes in their year.

The list really could go on and is dependent on where your curriculum is at this stage and the progression your subject leaders have made in their own leadership. It would be impossible to identify every step you could take in your school in this amount of space but one guiding principle is to help subject leaders become proactive: instead of just reflecting back on previous learning, look ahead to future content and give them space and time to provide teachers with content and direction for future teaching sequences.

Subject Leaders: Whether you are currently leading a subject or not at this stage, all teachers will likely have experience in leading a subject at some stage. Really, the aspects of good subject leadership have been outlined in the senior leaders' section above and in the explanation of how they need to enable that. However, let's say you are not in a school where subject leadership is prioritised and you are not given the direction.

Whilst you may not be able to access quality development in your own setting, there are numerous opportunities out there that are very low in cost. I would strongly recommend seeking out subject leader networks in your local area, subject associations linked with your subject and connected on Twitter with people who are also subject leads in your subject. You will be able to find a lot of support in these areas and they can give you places to start if you want to develop and champion your subject if the direction isn't being given in your own context.

You may also want to seek out further reading and materials focused on your subject. The *Primary Huh: Curriculum Conversations with Subject Leaders in Primary Schools (2022)* by Mary Myatt and John Tomsett is a great general place to begin. Subject-specific works are out there also and if you want to know where to begin in this huge journey, connecting with people on Twitter is your best place to start.

Problematic "Oven-Ready" schemes

For many of you, the above phrase "oven-ready" will bring back "fond" memories of a certain politician determinedly stating that the Brexit deal they had was ready to go and just needed to be voted through government. Aside from then suggesting we should stick it in the microwave (and the fact that the deal was anything other than oven-ready), the analogy was sound. The ability to pick up a product, prick it with a fork and stick it in the oven – ready to eat within a specified amount of time – would be a tantalising prospect for those who are time-poor. Of course, the nutritional values of these oven-ready meals compared to a home-cooked meal are questionable at best. They are often high in salt and fat because they must be made that way to be ready at any moment. Some are healthier than others but overall they do not provide the best that your body needs.

Teachers are very time-poor. As such, the rise of schemes that promise similar attributes to quick meals ("oven-ready" units of work) has been huge. They are ready to pick up and use with little preparation time. I, myself, have used a number of these schemes over the years I have taught. However, I have issue with these schemes or units for a number of reasons:

1. Generic nature – not applied to own school's context

    When someone sets out to produce a scheme of work that can be used by everyone else, this scheme will be very general. There will be little to no focus on the context of your school or the cultures that your class contains. Of course, an expert teacher will be able to take the scheme and adapt it to apply more to the children in their context. However, very often due to the lack of time teachers have, this personalisation of the curriculum won't take place. The scheme may be useful to give teachers ideas and a springboard into what direction they could take but caution would be needed.

2. Curriculum Coverage – do you know what it actually covers?

    After some time using some of these schemes, it occurred to me in a number of instances that there were things being covered that were not even in the National Curriculum!

    For example, the National Curriculum for Y6 Science states the following statutory expectations:

    Pupils should be taught to:

    - *recognise that light appears to travel in straight lines*
    - *use the idea that light travels in straight lines to explain that objects are seen because they give out or reflect light into the eye*

- *explain that we see things because light travels from light sources to our eyes or from light sources to objects and then to our eyes*
- *use the idea that light travels in straight lines to explain why shadows have the same shape as the objects that cast them (National Curriculum, 2015)*

A number of schemes I've looked at go further than this and go into aspects of light such as refraction. There is mention of this in the National Curriculum in the non-statutory area:

They could extend their experience of light by looking a range of phenomena including rainbows, colours on soap bubbles, objects looking bent in water, and coloured filters (they do not need to explain why these phenomena occur).

Looking through schemes that are available, lessons on refraction can end up going very in-depth into how refraction works, something which is specifically mentioned as not being necessary in the Primary Science curriculum. Precious time may be spent on that which could have been used to reinforce learning in other concepts or giving time to more objective-laden topics in that subject. Not every unit on every scheme will have this problem but it is one as an educator we should be aware of.

3. Fitting into your school's curriculum – is it the wrong shape?

Finally, as already outlined above, teachers need to be familiar with the curriculum that is on offer in a school. Often this may be demonstrated as key learning content of a document showing progression of skills across the school. If you are picking up and using a scheme from another site without carefully analysing the content, then there may be key learning that is missed which other teachers in the school are expecting you to have covered. Also, if you as a Year 6 teacher don't know which website or scheme the Year 4 teacher used to teach Electricity and there is no list of key learning objectives or knowledge that the school expects to be taught, then how are you meant to know their prior learning content? .

"Oven-ready" units of work are often seen as a quick method to delivering the content needed in a curriculum. However, the quality of the learning produced, along with the way it fits into the menu of your school curriculum, is not adequate for a nutritious and life-fulfilling learning diet. By all means, consider how to quickly source materials from such places – but as a teacher be the guide through these opportunities to provide quality learning experiences, rather than a distributor of facts and information.

Reflecting on the voices of primary education

■ What is the next step for your subject that you lead?

_____

_____

_____

_____

_____

_____

■ Are there any objectives you are teaching that could be removed that would give time to more important aspects that would have a bigger impact?

_____

_____

_____

_____

_____

_____

■ Are there items in your subject that you can be proactive about now to consider how to improve the curriculum offer?

_____

_____

_____

_____

_____

_____

The role of a curriculum coach

Tom Griffiths

The Education Inspection Framework has rightly put curriculum back at the heart of school inspections, with more time spent talking to pupils and staff about what they're learning. It's meant schools are ensuring their curriculum meets the needs of their children and community through the intent, implementation and impact of each subject and overall curriculum offered. As Kat Howard and Claire Hill mention in their book *Symbiosis: The Curriculum and The Classroom (2020)*, "we have to ensure the children in our care receive a rich, coherent and ambitious education that takes them beyond their own experiences so they can confidently meet the demands of whatever comes next." But what happens when, particularly in primaries, teachers are given a subject or subjects to lead when it is not their subject specialism?

Like other members of the Senior Leadership Team (SLT), I am lucky to work with incredible teachers who are in this boat and once the dreaded "O" word is uttered, you can see the worry and imposter syndrome sink in. What do you do to counter this and have an impact? Something we have been working on at my school over the past year or so is the role of the curriculum coach. We believe that there shouldn't just be one member of SLT designated as the "Curriculum Lead" as that is a lot of information for one person to hold and that can feel like a heavy responsibility (as well as workload); instead, all our executive leaders are curriculum coaches, allocated different subjects to support. The impact we've seen this academic year is vast: their confidence from our September inset (where each subject lead introduced their intent for this academic year) to July, where they presented their work during our Impact Day, was incredible to see. The following information revolves around the work the subject lead and myself did with History but this blueprint can easily be applied to the other curriculum subjects. In terms of context, we are a two-form entry maintained primary school with a leadership model of a Headteacher and three Assistant Headteachers (AHTs). The Headteacher and two of the AHTs are curriculum coaches, so I appreciate every school setting is different but I am positive there is a way this could work in your school.

So, what does it mean to be a curriculum coach?

It means working closely with the subject lead to enhance their subject. It does not mean making demands or simply telling them their next steps but instead, acting as a sounding board – listening to their problems and coaching them to find solutions and develop their confidence as a leader. By having a designated member of SLT supporting them, conversations can be picked up whenever appropriate and that subject lead knows whom to go with something, rather than going to their busy headteacher, who may have missed the context of previous conversations. In terms of experience, it also means that member of SLT can signpost the subject lead to places they may have been previously unaware of. One of the subjects I've been a coach for this year is History. Coaching the History lead has been very beneficial in enhancing my own continued professional development. The History lead's hard work and determination has meant she has finished the year knowing the clear impact all children have achieved from her subject. With limited non-contact time, it's been crucial as well to make the most of every opportunity.

So, what have we done since working together?

Building a curriculum takes time and the place we are now at is a journey which has taken us about 18 months. We all know there will never be a finished product – we can get it to a great point but then it will continue to evolve to reflect the changing needs of our school. What we started with was our intent: what does she want History to look like at our school? Why? One of the first thoughts was ensuring diversity in our History units. The local area has recently seen an extremely high number of pupils from Asia arriving so it was important for our intent to explore relevant historical periods for these pupils too. Once this intent was clear and her expectations were clear, we then looked at how this vision could be implemented.

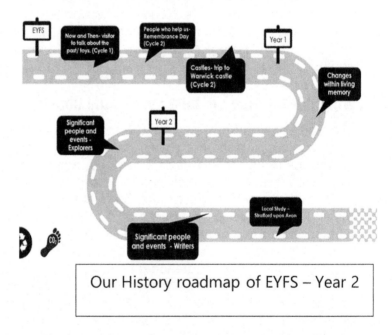

Our History roadmap of EYFS – Year 2

Through posing questions and next-step suggestions, the History lead was then able to review this subject's diet for a child going from EYFS to Year 6. First, we ensured we were meeting all National Curriculum objectives and then we moved on to the sequence of learning. When we looked at KS2, we noticed there was no clear chronology, so through coaching, the History lead went and investigated what she should do next. When I found relevant articles, I would send them to her and gradually, she developed a clear evidence-based reason why KS2 learning needed to be in chronological order. Furthermore, she was now confident explaining this – we realised previously that during our last curriculum review, we had let our writing objectives dictate where our History units were placed. To ensure key knowledge was embedded and progressed, this needed to change. Now, the learning journey for History is clear, sequenced and purposeful. This has helped us to plan enrichment opportunities across the year to support this learning now everything is opening up again in this COVID-19 era. As implementation has developed, the subject lead has now begun creating a curriculum map from EYFS to Year 6 covering key enquiry questions for each lesson, prior core knowledge, key vocabulary along with a brief lesson breakdown of key knowledge and skills to be taught and how to demonstrate impact. This is such a useful document for classroom teachers: it supports workload by having all the key information in one place, teachers can quickly recognise their children's prior learning and how their year group's learning fits into this journey.

Our next step has been around impact: how do we measure this? What retrieval opportunities can we use throughout lessons to build on prior learning? Where do cold and hot tasks fit into these conversations? This is where we are currently at and will continue to develop in the next academic year. Additionally, we are continuing to diversify our reading areas across all subjects and texts such as "Black and British: An Illustrated History" (David Olusoga) and "The Lion Above The Door" (Onjali Q. Raúf) have been a great starting point to support historical knowledge too.

When we had the opportunity to showcase History through a deep dive with our School Improvement Partner recently, I wanted this talented leader to have something to support them in case they get nervous and flustered. After seeing a resource created by Emma Stanley (@MissStanleyYr6) on Twitter and adapting it for myself as Maths lead, we sat down and I listened to her talk, creating her own "Subject on a Page" using these ideas. This document collates all the key information about the subject and our adviser loved it (as did the governors when I showed them my Maths one). If you get tongue-tied, you can refer to this and remind yourself. I know how much confidence it has given the History lead, and when during a recent CPD session she showed this to our teaching staff, they were keen to create one themselves for their own subjects.

Subject on a page

 Never Give Up

Intent: We aim to...

Ensure pupils gain a coherent knowledge and understanding of Britain's past and that of the wider world, whilst developing a strong sense of chronology.

Develop skills of critical thinking and inquiry by exploring Britain's past, our place in the world and how this has led to changes in the present day and future.

 Develop our pupils' awareness of what has shaped society and encourage them to become independent thinkers who form well-rounded opinions as responsible citizens.

Implementation: How do we achieve our aims?

 A cohesive curriculum

 Carefully sequenced lessons

 Reducing cognitive load

Ensuring coverage of the National Curriculum, we begin in EYFS looking at our own, personal history before moving onto history within our living memory in KS1. Here, we also explore significant people and events beyond living memory. Our approach is more chronology in KS2, exploring British and world history.

Our long term plan maps out lesson structures (e.g. timeline focus, sources/ artefacts and key people to be studied), with particular focus on chronology, causation and change throughout periods of history. This supports children with revisiting prior learning and enables them to build on and develop their existing knowledge and skills.

Our spiral curriculum ensures children are constantly revisiting and developing their knowledge further. As we have researched retrieval practice, we are mindful of cognitive overload. High quality teaching ensures PowerPoints and resources are relevant, not overly stimulated and focused on the learning.

Implementation (continued)

 Enrichment

We endeavour to provide the children with a purposeful trip or visitor as part of their learning. We believe this provides an immersive, memorable experience for the children and promotes the importance of history.

 Living History

We recognise that history does not stand still. Therefore, we aim to emphasise Living History through celebrating and commemorating key historical dates as a school, such as Remembrance Day, Black History Month and the Queen's Platinum Jubilee. Newsround and assemblies are vital for awareness of current events e.g. Ukraine/Russia.

Impact: How will we know we have achieved our aims?

By following the curriculum map, pupils are exposed to high quality, precise vocabulary, which allows them to understand abstract terms and make connections between time periods.

 Leaders use learning walks, lesson visits, pupil voice, data and book looks to assess and evaluate outcomes.

 Evidence-based, high quality CPD ensures staff are well-supported and can support all children effectively to make good progress.

Children are passionate and enthusiastic about History, often extending and sharing their learning at home.

Our 'Subject on a Page' for History

How have we made it work so effectively?

The key is to know your staff. If you don't know your team, you won't see those points where it's best to reschedule a meeting or limit the amount to be discussed before all our buckets overflow. As I've coached with the implementation of History, I've been excited by some of the articles I've read or people I've spoken to (thank you @Mr_S_History on Twitter for our little chats!) but then when I've gone to share this, I've noticed it isn't the right time for one reason or another and saved it for another time, where I know that information will be digested properly and thoughtfully. It's ensuring a culture of trust is created between the subject lead and curriculum coach. When Ofsted published their review series for History, I read it and forwarded it to my subject lead but also attached the brilliant notes I'd found on Twitter (thank you @MrMarcHayes). I suggested reading the notes first to get the key headlines and then when she had some appropriate time, read the rest.

Another reason we have made this work so effectively is our time management. We have got better at ensuring our meetings are recorded on our virtual calendars so we can't let anything interrupt us. We all know how busy school life is and it's so easy to say, "Let's just meet next week and we'll finish it." No, curriculum should be our priority so therefore it needs our focus. By dedicating this time and having a clear agenda, we are productive and this will impact our pupils.

Final thoughts

No matter where you are in your curriculum journey, the path ahead is daunting. Rome wasn't built in a day and neither will your curriculum. Break your plan into manageable chunks. With the majority of subject leads being classroom teachers and having limited non-contact time to work on their subject, it is important to have a clear port of call within your SLT. I highly recommend allocating subjects between your SLT and being curriculum coaches – it provides invaluable CPD for both parties, helps develop subject specialism and through coaching rather than simply delegating tasks, the subject lead still retains ownership of their subject and develops leadership qualities and confidence.

*Thank you to my History lead, Kirsty Tipper, for letting me share some of the work she has been doing this year. It's such a pleasure working with her and I've loved seeing her confidence and leadership skills develop further this year.

I am so grateful to Tom for contributing so valuably to this publication. He is an excellent Curriculum Lead and has really contemplated how to bring his subject leaders on the journey to developing the whole curriculum in his school. Readers may be subject leaders themselves or lead other subject leads but the principles of curriculum coaching outlined by Tom can support any educator in their development journey.

One of the things I love most about his contribution is how practical the insights are and just how anyone can pick up his ideas and apply them in some way to the work that they do.

Reflecting on the voices of primary education

■ What are areas of your current (or future) subject leadership that you want to develop?

_____

_____

_____

_____

_____

_____

■ What advantages do you see in a Curriculum Coach approach?

_____

_____

_____

_____

_____

_____

■ What development opportunities do you see from Tom's methodology that you can implement into your personal practice?

_____

_____

_____

_____

_____

Teaching and learning approaches

Ed Finch – @MrEFinch
Paul Watson – @PaulWat5

When compiling a volume like this of incredible voices from Primary Education, you can't help but love so many great ideas and insights that you hadn't considered before. Sometimes they slot well into an overarching theme – other times they are not so easy to pinpoint but are so valuable nonetheless. That is what this chapter is all about. In this chapter, you will find two highly respected colleagues from the edu-Twitter world who give their thoughts on what they do in the classroom to help teaching and learning of key content come to life in their own unique ways. You may well want to adopt some of the principles that they explain about in your own practice.

We will begin with Ed Finch who provides an absolute masterclass on how we need to seek out who we are as a teacher and lean into their tendencies and personalities to make our lessons sparkle with our unique characteristics. The way we approach teaching and learning will be formed from our authentic self and Ed talks wonderfully on this. We then move to Paul Watson who will share some fantastic models and examples on how he helps his learners become creators, not just consumers, and why this is an important shift to make in our teaching and learning.

DOI: 10.4324/9781003307150-4

Bringing your authentic self into the classroom

Ed Finch

Like so much in my life, I stumbled into teaching by mistake. Frustrated and exhausted with struggling to turn a shambolic string of theatre-related jobs, backed up by long days driving vans, into something resembling a career, I made snap decision to take a break from the whole thing. I'd go overseas and do something different just for a while and see if the hunger to make a living in acting and writing was still there when I got back.

A few months after that snap decision, I found myself in a small town, high up in the mountains, far to the north of Addis Abeba in the Tigray region of Ethiopia. I'd teach six classes a day, each with 80–100 pupils. I had a textbook, chalk and my wits. If I was going to survive the next two years of my life with my dignity intact, I was going to need to start making something happen pretty urgently.

Some of my students, the ones in the top sets, really wanted to learn. They thought they had a shot at being in the very top few per cent who get creamed off by the system to go to university, technical or college or into teaching. The students in any set below the top one knew the die was pretty well cast. They wouldn't be going to university or college. The best they could get was a certificate to show they had completed secondary education. That might get them an office job if there was one going but otherwise they were marking time.

I'd been counting on that old cliche "they're so eager to learn" to get me through but clearly that wasn't going to be enough. I was going to need to become a super teacher and fast.

Well, I told you that I'd been trying to make a living in the world of the theatre. Now was the time for that experience to pay off in the classroom. These students were going to be treated to the performance of their lifetimes – if that didn't make them start learning, then nothing would. And for that first few months I worked harder than I'd ever worked in my life. Not at becoming a better teacher but at acting like one. I didn't walk into the classroom, I made an entrance. I didn't give instructions – I declared them. I thought about the best teachers I'd had in my life – Mr Sayers, Miss Escolme, Mr Pace – and I stole bits of their schtick. A quizzical look that made you think again. A way of dropping the voice to make the students lean in. A way of pausing so the students had to finish a thought for themselves ....

If there were awards ceremonies for acting performances for pretending to be a teacher, I'd have been up for them. If there were awards ceremonies for being a teacher, however, I'd have been nowhere near. So much of my attention was going into this act of being a teacher that there was none left for really connecting with the pupils. When I set a regular quiz and almost none of the students could answer the simple questions I set, I was astonished and, frankly, angry. I'd done an amazing job of teaching that content, how dare they have failed to learn it.

I was rescued from this spiral by a lucky, lucky break. I was offered a place on a funded MA programme with Manchester Metropolitan University and started reading some research papers. I started reflecting on the social and political role of the teacher and got the very first inklings of an understanding that it isn't about the act you make of it – it's about the connections you make and the change you effect – and that you just aren't going to make those connections or effect that change if all your energy is going in to pretending to be someone you're not.

Hywel Roberts talks about a similar journey when he started teaching. He'd been very taken with Robin Williams performance as that inspirational teacher in Dead Poets Society. Hywel says that as a student teacher he had a still from the movie showing Williams' character being carried on the shoulders of his rejoicing students taped to the front of his file. His tutor was enraged by it and wrote across the picture in big pen "it's not about that." Hywel learned, as I did in my first year of teaching, that it's not about your amazing performance as a teacher, and it's not about applause or acclamation, it's about making a difference.

Don't get me wrong – I don't mean it's about touching hearts or healing broken minds. What our students need from us most of the time is good solid teaching so they have the skills, knowledge and, yes, qualifications to go on to the next step of what they need to do. They need to leave primary able to read and write and think and understand maths well enough to access the learning at big school. And in big school they need to learn the stuff they need to pass those GCSEs because, without those GCSEs they aren't going to get very much further. And, presuming they do get those GCSEs, they need to get those A-levels and they need to get the grades to access whatever is next. The biggest difference we can make is to ensure our students get the skills and knowledge they need to access their next step and very often that gets expressed in terms of qualifications.

For a lot of our pupils, this is the role that we play in their lives. Some will forget us entirely – "What was the name of that man who taught us in Year 7? You must remember him – he had a beard – he taught French …. Other students might have particular reasons to remember us – "Of course I remember him – I ran into him in Sainsbury's once and he made my little brother stop crying and laugh by doing a trick with his ears." And for others, the reasons might be deeper – "he spoke to me after my mum died and he showed me he really understood." All of these positions are fine – we don't need to be remembered any more than the mechanic who fixes my car needs to be remembered – if we do some extra good in the world as we pass through it, that is extra good.

The point I'm labouring towards is not that we need to touch lives in some mystical way – it's that to do the basic job of teaching really well, we need to be authentically ourselves in the classroom. That the job is too important and too complex for us to be able to waste energy on pretending to be someone else or something we are not.

Why was I, back in the early months of my teaching career in that high school in Ethiopia, surprised when my students couldn't answer the questions in my quizzes? Surely that shouldn't have been unexpected? The truth was that I just hadn't been listening. Sure I'd cocked my head to one side, or looked quizzical, or paused to let them finish the thought themselves but all that had been projection, and if you aren't sucking information in as a teacher, you aren't going to be making informed decisions about what to do next.

This is why I always get a bit worried when people say teaching is "all performance" or advise students to "fake it till you make it." It mistakes the performance of teaching with the actual substance of the job. The bit that makes the difference between someone pretending to be a teacher and someone actually doing the job.

One of my students was angry a lot of the time. He'd call out and pretty much heckle me through lessons. He could time it so an explanation was sabotaged just at the wrong moment and I'd have to go back to the beginning and I'd have to start again. Very frustrating.

Another pupil gave the impression of being extremely bright but failed quiz after quiz after quiz. Was she just not listening to me?

When I was able to slow right down, to stop myself being angry and to start to listen and be present, I started to notice things. My angry student seemed different somehow. He dressed differently from the other pupils and carried himself differently too. I spoke to him and learned how his family were from over the border in Eritrea, the two countries were at war, his father and brother were at the front and he hadn't heard from them in weeks, he was worried and angry, people who should have known better were treating him with suspicion because his family were "the enemy." He was on his own and lonely and scared. And so used to being treated as a bad boy that he'd accepted he might as well play the part.

I slowed down and took an interest in my apparently bright pupil; I took a proper look at her work – not easy to commit to when you have 600 pupils in a week but still a shocking admission for a teacher to make. Some of her words had the right letters in the wrong order, some were just a scramble. She could answer any question verbally, but clearly there was something stopping her from getting it written down. I'd heard of dyslexia, might she be dyslexic?

Once I started to leave the performance out of the classroom, a barrier fell away and I could attend to the atmosphere in the room, the answers the pupils gave, the clues they gave me as to their motivation and understanding. I could better predict what the difficult bits of a lesson were going to be, where I'd need to break things down into smaller steps. What I could safely assume was securely learned and where I'd need to check the ground ahead of me.

Let's look at feedback – lots of schools have dropped their marking policies and adopted feedback policies in their places, but I think in a lot of places this is assumed to mean what we feed back to the pupils. This could be marking in books and might even be dialogical marking, I suppose a verbal feedback stamp might conceivably be involved or maybe it really is that, in the moment, over-the-shoulder correction of a misconception. But shall we turn it around and ask if the feedback could be what we are getting back from the pupils – what we are learning about the effect of our teaching on them. What does feedback look like in your classroom? Does it look like you reminding the children that an adverbial phrase at the start of a sentence needs to be demarcated with a comma before the main clause or does it look like you listening, considering and learning why the brilliant explanation you toiled over last week somehow didn't actually teach them the one bit you thought it was going to. When you are authentically yourself in the classroom, there's a little bit more room for humility and a little more room for taking the feedback from the learners.

There's a lot of talk in teaching at the moment about the basic tools of teaching – great modelling, great questioning and great feedback. These foundation blocks of the job are being defined as never before with multiple books being published and schemes for instructional coaching being developed to help us all – new teachers and more experienced teachers alike – get better at the basics. And we can all get better. But make no mistake, none of these books and none of this coaching is going to have much effect if you aren't able to be authentically yourself in the classroom. You will model more clearly if you are open to accepting how the learners receive it, you will ask better questions if you are genuinely interested in the answers, you will give feedback if you are open to that being a two-way process.

Making a difference to a young person's life means making sure that they can take the next step. I believe that we will be able to do that far more effectively if we stop pretending to be teachers and start really being our empathetic, connection seeking and human selves.

When I was starting out as a teacher half my lifetime ago, in a high school in the mountains of Ethiopia, I thought back to my best teachers, Geoff Sayers, Bridgette Escolme, Jonathan Pace, and tried to use their tricks to make my performance more convincing. I'm older now and looking back I think I've put my finger on the actual reasons that they were so good. Turns out it wasn't their tricks after all, it's because they were genuinely interested in me and my learning. Unless they were just VERY good at pretending ....

Ed is another one of those personalities on Twitter who when I began scouting out early guests for the podcast, his name came up a lot. He talks a lot of sense about primary education, and when we did meet for the podcast, it was clear to see the passion he has for the role that we play in the lives of young people.

When considering teaching and learning, there are libraries worth of books and resources that point you to the next, evidence-informed practice that represents the "best bets" for children's education. However, when I thought back over the growing catalogue of Primary Education Voices interviews that have taken place, Ed's views on, first and foremost, bringing your authentic self to the classroom were insightful and sage.

It reminds me of being an NQT (the "old" version of an ECT!) and observing other teachers teach. One misconception I took away was that their classes were behaving impeccably for these teachers because of the way they "performed." I thought that if I just acted the way they did, said that explanation the way they did, then I would have my class eating out of the palm of my hand. What happened afterwards was the opposite: I felt awkward, my class felt confused and engagement in my class worsened.

What I needed to do was analyse WHAT my colleagues did, not HOW. For sure, there are approaches and strategies that are found to be more effective in enhancing teaching and learning in the classroom. However, finding your style of delivery and how you interact with your class is one of the subtle secrets of education. Find that and you will see that children will respond much better to your authentic self – no matter what that self may be – and you will be less focused on how you are doing things and be able to focus more on the learning taking place.

Reflecting on the voices of primary education

■ Think of a teacher (from your own education or a colleague) that inspired you – what about them inspired you?

_____

_____

_____

_____

_____

_____

■ How would a learner in your class describe you as a teacher?

_____

_____

_____

_____

_____

■ Are there any gaps between the teacher you are presenting yourself as and the person you actually are?

_____

_____

_____

_____

_____

Children being creators, not consumers

Paul Watson

Creators, not consumers – it is a term I thought I coined, but most likely stole it from someone far more knowledgeable than myself. In fact, I now know I did. Like all consumers, I took on various ideas from a range of sources without creating content of my own; my own thoughts and ideas of my daily pursuit of teaching. That is not to say I never made worksheets, or wrote laborious lesson plans that I didn't look at during a lesson, I just didn't have the knowledge or understanding of the true outcomes I wanted to achieve.

In my initial teaching career, I was a consumer of schemes of work, of photocopied sheets, of planning from the drive that was completed by past teachers, and it meant the learning of my classes was not as sharp as it should be. In fact, the outcomes were a rouges gallery of poor proxies. Completed work that was marked – check. Labelled worksheets to show learning – check. Coverage of the curriculum completed – check. Remembering the knowledge over an extended period – not quite.

An Ethics of Excellence by Ron Berger (2003) was the game changer. You may not have heard of Ron and his fantastic book on teaching, but you most likely will have come across Austin's Butterfly. For those of you still in the dark, Austin drew a rather rubbish butterfly but through constructive feedback and repeated attempts, his artwork flourished into an impressive butterfly that any child could be proud of. This was just one aspect of Berger's work, with elements such as real purpose, craftsmanship and individuality at the core of how he managed to facilitate his learners to learn more, and most importantly, create more.

Ensuring that my learners began to learn more, remember more and be able to use that knowledge to create more became a true pursuit. The selection of what I know and view as important as well as how I choose to share it with others is the apex of thinking deeply. As Daniel T. Willingham said: "Memory is the residue of thought," and making children really think matters. Thinking back to my previous teaching, it was hoop jumping for the children. Shallow learning. Task completion. Not quite good enough to be honest. It was time for a change.

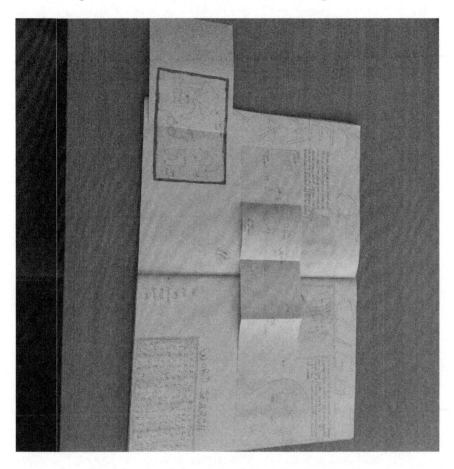

I decided to develop an approach in history and geography that taught knowledge in a very direct way, yet placed the emphasis on the pupils to decide how they presented that knowledge at the end point of their learning. As you can see in the examples above, the children could take the same information – in this case the work of the Montgolfier brothers – and incorporate their own ideas to share their learning. This led to work that was individual and to the children remembering more, as they had to make choices on what to include, why and how to present it. In short, they had to think deeper about the concepts they were being taught.

This often takes the form of double-page spreads as it allows the children to present more learning, in a manner that they feel fit. Why a double-page spread you may ask? Well, simply providing more space means the learners have a clear challenge to produce more content. At first, children will opt to work "bigger" by adding a title that dominates or illustrations that fill the space. This is when modelling and clear expectations come into play. I tend to place the types of pages produced into two categories: directed and free form. Directed pages are, as the name suggests, where the content and much of the layout are decided for and modelled to the children. Backgrounds can be printed to speed up the process and paragraphs produced as a part of a writing unit with a clear sequence. Illustrations would be the only aspect the children had an option on, with some opting for digital art and others watercolours in these directed pages.

Pre-teaching content is a major step to consider. We cannot expect children to know things they have yet to be taught, which places the emphasis on the teacher to ensure that the content the children create is packed with accurate knowledge. How do we ensure the children know what we need them to know? This is when straightforward, traditional, closed procedure tasks such as completing diagrams do prove to be useful as a means of direct instruction, as well as exposing them to high-quality non-fiction texts, ideally slightly above their own reading age. However, in isolation these tasks don't encourage deeper thinking about the content.

Working to deadlines becomes a skill that children develop when working in this manner. As each outcome is slightly different and the way in which each child works, the need for clear deadlines is a must. Perfectionists and work racers need to adapt the most to becoming creators for very different reasons. The perfectionist will take forever, tear up failed efforts and never quite be satisfied and become in danger of falling behind, while work racers complete their work by lowering their personal standards, as they value completion over quality.

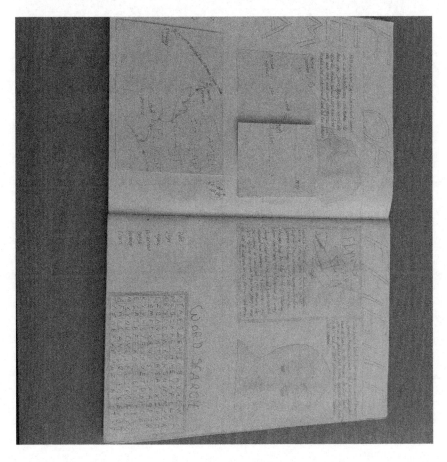

Both types of learners do adapt over time and this prepares them well for later in their learning journey when more independence is placed upon them.

Collaboration is key. When it came to the sharing of good ideas, it was actively encouraged to "steal" an idea from a peer.

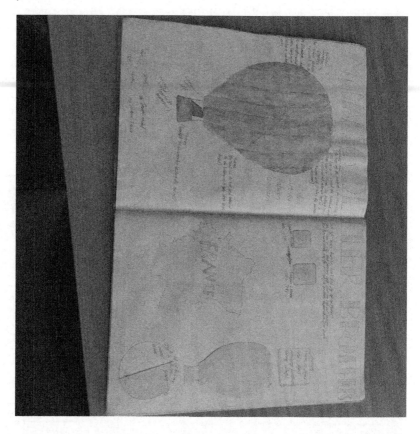

Praise in public is a great motto to have in teaching and what it allows a teacher to do is direct other learners to exemplars. Feedback doesn't always have to be constructive feedback with an aspect to improve; it can and often should be the verbal recognition of outstanding thinking. In an organic manner, and with no moaning from the original creators due to the learning climate, children either decided to come up with a "new" way to present it, or followed the examples and attempted their own versions. The same map, presenting the same information, yet multiple ways employed by the learners to present to their audience.

Craftsmanship often becomes a concern for some when adopting this approach. Questioning if the time spent on creating beautiful work is worth it, or in fact detracts from the learning. My personal view, as biased as it is, is that the children take real pride from it, spend far longer considering what they have learned and apply other aspects of the wider curriculum such as art, digital literacy and DT. What about time wasted when I should be teaching x, y and z? First you have to ask if x, y and z really do need teaching and, if so, to what extent. Put simply, a curriculum breaking under the weight of too much to cover is not fit for purpose. Once you free yourself from the shackles of having to teach with constraints, be it time or far too many learning objectives, then you are able to teach better. Second, there is a very real point around the need to develop "analogue" skills. The ability to hand draw a map, or work in a methodical, neat manner, or even to colour in and cut out with a degree of confidence and accuracy – if your class can't do these things well, then you have to ask yourself why not? Most likely, because it isn't important to you until you need them to display such skills and get frustrated at their inability to do something you've not allowed them to do on a regular basis. In a digital age, we need our children to still adapt to being able to work with real materials.

I must point out that double-page spreads are my preference when developing a curriculum that encourages the children to become creators. There are many ways you can do this such as through well-thought-out presentations in which the children decide on the content and their viewpoint, or digital workbooks that deploy a multimedia approach, including audio and video clips. The whole point of this approach is about taking the ball and running with it. I encourage teachers to do this and create their own ways that work in their settings and contexts.

To try and explain why this approach is better than others, I tend to reflect on writing moderation in primary schools. If I'm presented with a pile of books to moderate, I start by reading the work. In a class of 30, most children will all write the same story with the same plot, so it would be wrong to expect vastly different work. However, if each child produces the same story, written in the same way to the point in which it feels like you have read the same thing over and over and over, then you would have to come to the conclusion that the teacher has scaffolded far too much. This is what happens in many of our wider foundation lessons: each child produces the same work. We accept it as we feel rushed when it comes to geography, history, art and DT. And in doing so, we take the less rewarding route for our learners.

At the start of the piece, I mentioned that I didn't coin the phrase "creators, not consumers" and merely stole it. Mary Myatt wrote a fantastic blog (https://www.marymyatt.com/blog/creators-not-consumers) stating her views on the matter with far more panache than me.

I determined that Paul was an absolute must when I thought about putting this book together. The discussion we had about children being creators has drawn a number of positive comments. For me, it bridges the gap between making our curriculums more focused on knowledge and exploring ways of making learning "stick" more whilst still providing creative ways for them to present this and build skills of application and discussion.

One thing I love from Paul's entry here is how he likens the difference between a creator and a consumer in the classroom to us as teachers being either creators or consumers. I am confident that each of us can relate to times where we have clicked download for a scheme of work from a generic resource site and then delivered the contents of that scheme as prescribed in the materials. Was there coverage for the curriculum? Maybe (I refer you back to my entry in Chapter 3). Were the children engaged? Possibly – although I contend that it is very difficult to achieve this. The reason why for that is because if you have downloaded and distributed a ready-made resource that is part of a wider scheme that again you have sourced from elsewhere, you are less likely to have the passion and knowledge about its contents. Now, please do not misunderstand me, sometimes a ready-made lesson is perfectly adequate and fits in well with the curriculum you are delivering. In fact, it can give you space and time to think more deeply about the direction you want your curriculum to take the children and the objectives that you want to cover whilst providing plenty of opportunities to review prior and taught learning content. What I think that Paul is suggesting here and I am stating is that mass-downloading an entire scheme of learning, without thinking about the objectives being covered behind it and how it fits into your wider school curriculum is the problematic practice here and something which the Internet – as powerful a tool as it is for developing teaching and learning it is – has laid out one avenue for us to follow.

As such, Paul's implication that we as teachers must become creators, not consumers, is powerful. Not necessarily that we painstakingly produce every worksheet or handcraft every presentation file but that we are deliberate about the content, delivery method and learning opportunities that we include. This, for me, was insightful.

I hope that you appreciate Paul's willingness to share perceptions from his practice and indeed real examples from his classroom. His direction to guide children to become creators, I really think, is something that all primary educators should consider integrating into their practice. He mentioned in his podcast interview that this would not be for every subject every half term but a learning style that would be used in a couple of places during the half term to give children the chance to develop wider skills and application. I loved the point he made that when children move into secondary education and into the wider world that they will need skills such as independence and innovation to stand out. Scaffolding how and supporting them to become creators, not just consumers, is a great way to sow those seeds.

Reflecting on the voices of primary education

■ What benefits do you identify from this approach to empower children to become creators?

_____

_____

_____

■ What principles would you take from the discussion to make sure this works as an approach in your classroom?

_____

_____

_____

■ What subject areas/content could you apply this to in the next term?

_____

_____

_____

_____

_____

5

Developing as an educator

Adam Woodward – @adamjames317
Bryony Turford – @priscigeeks

Over the past number of years, there has been an explosion of educational resources at the fingertips of teachers. Well-researched and informative practices and insights are now more available than ever, and in a profession where one moment you are teaching the intricacies of the English language and then the next you are wielding some oil pastels to create majestic pieces of art (and everything else I could list), these insights and ideas couldn't be more welcome! The following contributors will share their expertise in the area of developing ourselves as educators.

First, Adam Woodward shares his brilliant thoughts around the world of educational research. For some, this may be a daunting arena but he shares ways to get involved and how he has started his journey into become more evidence-informed and the impact this has had in his classroom. After that, we will then have Bryony Turford who is another excellent educator to include in this work. She shares the value of subject-specific training to improve our subject knowledge and how, no matter your own areas to develop, you can address those quickly with the resources on offer – and often for a very small cost!

Research-informed teaching and learning

Adam Woodward

Since the world changed, the UK moved into lockdown and schools moved towards a remote learning model of teaching, I found myself engaging more with the world of #EduTwitter and, as such, was pointed in the direction of more educational research. As I started to access more blogs, books, podcasts and research articles, a new world was opened up to me that I had not engaged with previously – the world of evidence-informed practices. Now, I had access to the minds and words of those people who had used their own practice and those of others within teaching to further my own professional development.

At first, it can be quite overwhelming – where do you start? Since 2014, there has been an explosion in educational research and there is now so much choice and many different directions to take on developing your pedagogical approaches to your own teaching practice.

My starting point coincided with an interview for a senior leadership role at my school. As a part of my direction for my vision for our school, I came across the blogs of Tom Sherrington and the research of Kate Jones on retrieval practice. Both expert educators who have had an enormous impact on my own practice. Sherrington's writing on curriculum development led me towards Rosenshine's Principles in Action – the ideal starting point for anyone wanting to improve their classroom practice. This naturally signposted me to other research papers and educators and thus, a passion for evidence-informed practice took a hold of me!

Since this moment, my CPD library has grown and my knowledge and understanding of classroom and whole school pedagogy have too. This led me to want to use my senior position in my school to share what I had read and support teaching and learning as well as the development of teachers' practice. This started with a staff meeting on retrieval practice and the benefits of this within the curriculum, on cognitive load and long-term memory. The next two terms would be used to implement a series of different templates to "retrieve" core knowledge from prior learning and to embed learning into the long-term memory. We used examples of retrieval practice within our history and geography lessons to begin with and came together to evaluate their impact, support each other and for teachers to champion its use within our curriculum.

The introduction of retrieval practice in our school was supported by my creation of knowledge organisers. In recent years, knowledge organisers have been the subject of many conversations around the subject of retrieval practice and its implementation both in primary and secondary schools. The term was first coined by Joe Kirby in 2015 as "the most awesome tool in the arsenal of the curriculum designer ... These organise all the most vital, useful and powerful knowledge on a singular page." This focus was primarily based around their inclusion for secondary students as a form of independent study and revision for GCSE and A-Level students but the conversation since then has also been as to whether they could be implemented in the primary setting.

In primary, knowledge organisers are a great tool for teachers in the classroom when it comes to planning, teaching and assessment. However, children need to be given the opportunity to engage with them. One way of supporting this outside the classroom is by sharing them with parents. The way that we have done that in my setting is, at the beginning of each term, our knowledge organisers are sent to parents via our school bulletin with a preamble as to what they are and how they can be used effectively to support the learning of the children. We also state how parents can be supporting the acquiring of key knowledge with their children themselves. What this sharing of knowledge organisers also achieves is a communication with parents as to what is being taught in the classroom. It promotes revision techniques as we ask for these to be printed, pinned to the fridge or bedroom wall and it also promotes discussion around the dining table. In a world dominated by screens and digital media, we see this as a great way for children (and parents) to demonstrate their knowledge and understanding of a unit.

As the contributor mentions, knowledge organisers are in effect one-page summaries of the unit that they cover. Key items of knowledge that the teacher or subject leader would hope that the children would engage with can be found there and they can be used for several purposes across the school in teaching and learning.

One function they accomplish that I am particularly keen on investigating myself is how they support subject leaders in making clear to the teachers that teach their subject what content is "expected" to be taught in that unit. Too often, as an admin on a Year 3/4 Facebook group which welcomes over 30,000 practitioners, I see people asking for planning that covers entire units on "Natural Disasters" or "Romans" and I do have to wonder if these teachers would be better supported if their subject leaders outlined the actual content that they needed to teach. Of course, a knowledge organiser will not cover the entirety of the intended curriculum (it would be impossible to do so on one engaging page) but it would be a valuable resource.

There are some fantastic resources out there in the edu-world about the theory behind knowledge organisers and some practical resources in using them also. Just one Google search will lead you to plenty of research that cites their potential but having said that, as with all educational research, stark warnings. For knowledge organisers, that includes not teaching children the metacognitive strategies to use them to their potential and not having a coherent curriculum in place. As Adam continues, exploring the research will only make us better educators.

As I stated above, this was my starting point in the world of evidence-informed practice to provide a positive impact on the outcomes for teaching and learning across the school. I have since continued to provide teachers in my setting with signposts to further improve their practice. Each half term, I have produced a summary of good practice in the form of a teaching and learning newsletter that focuses on one area of evidence-informed research for teachers to engage with. Examples of such include Tom Sherrington's "Rosenshine's Principles in Action," Kate Jones' "Retrieval Practice" series of books and Mary Myatt's "Back on Track," all designed with evidence-informed practice at their heart to improve teaching and learning in all areas of the school.

This has culminated in being a part of a team across my school that introduced Tom Sherrington and Oliver Caviglioli's Walkthrus programme to further support teachers – and teaching assistants – in improving their pedagogical approaches to teaching and learning.

As a school, we have worked together to form a solid foundation for teachers to work from, ensuring that we work to their strengths and to build upon these, working collaboratively to learn from each other and knowing that "We want to create a culture where every teacher believes they need to improve, not because they are not good enough, but because they can be even better ..." (Dylan Wiliam).

As a takeaway from this, some thoughts to ask of yourself and the other teachers within your setting would be:

1. What strengths do your teachers hold that could be used across the school to support the teaching and learning of everyone.
2. In what ways can you share good practice with the rest of your school? In the form of a termly newsletter to sign-post teachers in the right direction, as seen above, could be just one example.
3. When introducing an evidence-informed approach into school, have you considered the "why?" How will the introduction of this benefit the teaching and learning across the school?

I would like to finish on promoting the tireless work of educators that I have been fortunate enough to come across and take inspiration from my relatively short foray into the world of evidence-informed practice. Most notably Kate Jones, whose research into retrieval practice and the role that cognitive science plays in this, has had a huge impact on my practice.

My commute into work has also changed for the better thanks to the Thinking Deeply about Primary Education podcast produced by Kieran Mackle. If you are yet to come across this, and have an interest in evidence-informed practices, then this is a must-listen. From marking to planning, from curriculum design to SEND practices, there is something for everyone here.

The work of Tom Sherrington, Neil Almond and Clare Sealy on curriculum design has also re-evaluated my approach within my role. Learning from them via their blogs on the subject, talks at researchED and implementation of their approaches is of a huge benefit to curriculum leaders and I am forever grateful for their generosity in sharing their expertise.

There are countless other members of the education community and #EduTwitter who provide such great insights into education and how we can have a positive impact on teaching and learning as leaders and practitioners. I can only apologise to those who I have been unable to mention here but the above are great starting points that will signpost you into the right directions, just as they have done myself.

Adam is another great voice to add to this fantastic group of primary educators and the resources and materials he cites are all the foundations of an excellent beginning to get stuck into this wonderful world of research-informed practice. His newsletter idea for his staff is an excellent one and if you are interested to find out more about that I'd strongly recommend that you get in touch with him. In fact, just follow him on Twitter and you will find he is a great signposter to all sorts of current updates and resources for the classroom.

Reflecting on the voices of primary education

■ How much would you say you have engaged with educational research?

_____

_____

_____

_____

_____

_____

■ What area of your practice would you like to develop further?

_____

_____

_____

_____

_____

_____

<hr>

■ What are some of the resources listed by Adam that you will look into further?

_____

_____

_____

_____

_____

_____

<hr>

Developing your own subject knowledge through networking

Bryony Turford

When was the last time you had some specific professional learning to develop your subject knowledge? Last week? Last month? Last year? Many years ago, or perhaps never.

How good was that professional learning? How did it impact on you? How did it impact on your colleagues? How did you share what you learned?

Did you network with other colleagues as part of that professional learning? Did you make some connections that lasted longer than the activity? What part did they play in developing your subject knowledge?

What about the children? Ultimately, if an episode of professional learning is going to be an effective one and moves us on as teachers, it should impact on pupils and their learning in the classroom. Otherwise, what is the point?

In primary schools today, many of us, without subject-specific qualifications, are expected to lead subjects, support the subject knowledge development of colleagues and be ultimately responsible for the quality of teaching and learning of our subjects. This is the same level of scrutiny as our secondary colleagues, many of whom have degree level subject knowledge in the subjects they are teaching and leading. I have worked with several primary colleagues who are leading subjects they don't even teach; such is the nature of the curriculum beast at primary level in the current climate. The purpose of this section is not to discuss the validity of this approach. In fact, I personally welcome the renewed focus on the wider curriculum, but how and where can we go about upskilling ourselves in subject knowledge, specifically through networking?

I am going to share a range of ways you can develop your own subject knowledge. As someone who has a key role in developing professional learning in primary science almost all of the time, I am extremely passionate about the value of the network I am surrounded by and the networks I seek to create with the teachers I work with. I will exemplify these opportunities through the primary science lens.

Social media

For me, this is mainly Twitter and Facebook. I use Twitter to share ideas, retweet those of others and like and comment on threads, discussing all things primary and particularly science. I have been on Twitter as @PriSciGeeks for nearly 10 years and have curated my timeline carefully to ensure it stays positive and full of great teachers and ideas for sharing. On Facebook, I am a member of several of the primary science groups and often respond to comments and questions as well as post resources and ideas I have found elsewhere. If you are new to social media as an educator or as a subject leader, make sure you start with connecting to legitimate organisations such as subject associations first and then searching out specialists in that field and following them. I was amazed at how many people whose books I have read or whose resources I use are on Twitter and are always happy to engage in conversation. I have gained so much from being a part of this network.

School-to-school subject networks

School-to-school subject networks have their origins in termly subject leader networks associated with the Local Authority structure. The creation of Multi Academy Trusts (MATs) has redrawn the county or borough boundaries for many of us and our immersion in online CPD and meetings since the COVID-19 pandemic in 2020 has left us realising that long car journeys, the inevitable sprint out of the door at the end of the meeting for a staff meeting or to collect our own children is not always needed. The virtual world has created a range of CPD opportunities where new subject knowledge can be gained and links made hundreds of miles away, or even internationally. I wonder how many of such meetings are about building strong networks though. As a provider of CPD and a range of networking opportunities as part of my job, I try hard to ensure breakout rooms are effective, useful and fruitful but that isn't always possible no matter how well-intentioned. The real networking is done around the coffee machine in the break or in the lull before the sessions start – the buzz in the room is palpable when networks who already know each other reconvene. But what if you are new? What if you are attending something new? What if no one talks to you? Use the network leader, ask them to introduce you to someone who you could pair up with and connect with. If you are a regular attender, sit next to someone you don't normally chat with, spot someone new and make them feel welcome. Make sure you connect on social media or via email so connections can be nurtured after the initial event. These network events often have a more sharing focus than delivery of content but can still be a great place to learn new things that develop your subject knowledge and can be shared with colleagues in school easily.

Subject associations

As long-time member of the Association for Science Education (ASE), I cannot advocate for association membership enough. I can't imagine how I could have done my job as a science leader without it, and I certainly would not have had the career opportunities I have had and continue to have without it. The conferences, regional activity, welcoming members who are now my colleagues and friends have all been essential to my development as a leader of science and now a facilitator, CPD leader and champion for subject leaders. The openness and sharing nature of the ASE left me stunned at first. I was made to feel special and valued from my very first event. The dedicated volunteers are so keen to share their knowledge and I have developed in terms of pedagogy, subject knowledge, skills, finding new resources and even gone on to collaborate and create resources of my own. Without that network, I would not have had the confidence, belief or knowledge of where to even start. I knew I quite liked teaching science and was enjoying leading it but finding the ASE took this to a whole new level. I am lucky enough to be working with many of the other subject associations now and find them all to be as warm and friendly as my first encounter with ASE. If you are not yet a member of your subject association, I firmly believe it should be an entitlement of all primary leaders. Your subject association is there for you as a leader and that should always be your starting point for subject knowledge and connections.

Subject-specific professional learning

I have placed this strand separately from networks as this has a more specific focus. In a science context, this might involve some CPD around a particular area of science teaching such as physics in lower key stage 2 (7- to 9-year-olds) or learning about active assessment strategies for elicitation in primary science. More often referred to as a "course," these can be anything from a couple of hours to a residential over an extended period. The longer the course or programme, the more networking opportunities will arise. For example, the national STEM learning centre runs courses that can be up to 9 days, with three lots of 3-day residential periods over 6 months. Another primary science example is an Education Endowment Foundation (EEF) trial I am working on called "Thinking, Doing, Talking Science." This programme is a 4-and-a-half-day programme over 10 months where delegates meet together to learn about aspects of the approach, go back to their schools, try things out, work with colleagues and then return to the next session to share their reflections and hear from others. This opportunity for intensive subject-specific periods of learning with peers, time back in your own school to get to grips with new knowledge, approaches and resources before reconvening and building on this again, is a powerful way to build knowledge as a community, doing it together and supporting each other on that way. National programme such as National Professional Qualification in Leading Teaching (NPQLT) is another example of this networking as are many other subject-specific approaches.

Subject development programmes and awards

Lots of subject associations and organisations have these – History Quality Mark, Geography Quality Mark, Arts Mark, for example. For many years, I have been closely involved with the Primary Science Quality Mark (PSQM) where schools undertake a year-long programme of subject development based on key identified development needs and work with a local hub leader and other schools to undertake this development. This particular programme is much wider than subject knowledge, but that is partly why I have included it. Considering subject knowledge within a wider development plan for that subject is more likely to make the choices of which networking connections need nurturing; what can be parked for a while and what needs a refresher. It is more likely to be targeted around the needs of the school, the educator and the children, and therefore should have greater impact if it meets a recognised need. Taking part in any of these programmes is about the whole school and requires support from the school leadership to drive forward with a vision and commitment to developing a particular subject. When they are left in the hands of one individual no matter how great the programme is, it is neither sustainable nor embedded in the ethos of subject teaching and learning. When there is a whole school commitment and focus, it can be transformational and long term.

So what?

The most significant question you should ask yourself about any of the networking connections you are making to develop subject knowledge is "so what?" Taking valuable time out of the classroom during the teaching day, your own time after school, at the weekend or perhaps extended residential periods all take time to organise, plan and manage. If this does not make a difference to your subject knowledge, and ultimately to the quality of teaching and the quality of learning, then what was the point? Sometimes, that impact is not immediately obvious, it needs time to sink in and simmer, to assimilate, to chat, to read more, and ultimately, to explore those connections. Other times, things might be immediate, takeaways, do tomorrow and are a quick win.

When considering a networking opportunity, you might want to consider:

- What is my need?
- Does this networking opportunity support or develop my need?
- Can I support or develop the needs of others with this opportunity?
- What do I want to get out of it?

When returning from a networking opportunity, you might want to consider:

- Was my need met in the short term?
- Who do I want to talk to in my own school as a result of that opportunity?
- What do I want to do or try in the short term (in the next fortnight)?
- What about the medium term (the next term)?
- What about in the longer term (the next year)?

Arriving at an event or resource with a clear idea of what you want to achieve is always a good plan. Equally, networking for the sake of networking can bring about the most natural of connections. A need you didn't know you had until you started chatting to someone else is where some of the most creative ideas can arise – meeting someone who thinks like you or has a different perspective is always such a joyous part of the ongoing learning that is our profession. We've learned so much from our forced online networking. We are loving being back in a room with real people and the blended future is as exciting as it has ever been.

Recommendations

Reading

Effective Professional Development guidance report from Education Endowment Foundation (EEF), https://educationendowmentfoundation.org.uk/education-evidence/guidance-reports/effective-professional-development

Guskey's five critical levels of professional development evaluation, https://educationendowmentfoundation.org.uk/education-evidence/guidance-reports/effective-professional-development

Turford, B. and Bianchi, L. (2021). The right CPD for the right teacher at the right time. ASE Primary Science Journal. 167, 28.

Mary Myatt – Back on Track and The Curriculum – Gallimaufry to coherence. Each of these books has subject-specific chapters in them with great ideas for leading your subject but also great places to start making your subject-specific connections.

I would also recommend signing up for her weekly three things for Thursday newsletter – something to read, listen to and to watch. For bitesize CPD and keeping you connected to the wider education network, visit https://www.marymyatt.com/myatt-co

Subject development awards

Arts Mark, https://www.artsmark.org.uk/

Primary Geography Quality Mark, https://www.geography.org.uk/The-Primary-Geography-Quality-Mark-PGQM

Primary History Quality Mark, https://www.history.org.uk/primary/categories/quality-mark

Primary Science Quality Mark, http://www.psqm.org.uk/

Space Education Quality Mark, https://www.stem.org.uk/esero/space-education-quality-mark

Twitter Primary Science starting points

@PriSciGeeks @Glazgow @SIMMSPriScience @PSQM_HQ @theASE @PSTT_whyhow @UoMSEERIH

Subject Associations

Art – National Society for Education in Art and Design, https://www.nsead.org/

Computing – computing at school, https://www.computingatschool.org.uk/

Design Technology – The Design and Technology Association, https://www.data.org.uk/

Geography – Geographical Association, https://www.geography.org.uk/

History – Historical Association, https://www.history.org.uk/

MFL – Association for Language Learning, https://www.all-languages.org.uk/

Music - Music Mark, https://www.musicmark.org.uk/
PE – Association for Physical Education, https://www.afpe.org.uk/physical-education/
PSHE – PSHE Association, https://pshe-association.org.uk/
RE – National Association of Teachers of Religious Education, https://www.natre.org.uk/
Science – Association of Science Education, https://www.ase.org.uk/

It is no secret that one of the keys to effective teaching and learning is strong subject knowledge. Whenever you are standing in front of a class of children and the lesson takes a turn you were not expecting, having a solid foundation of subject knowledge to work from is vital and makes the difference between embedding knowledge or inadvertently promoting misconceptions. The unique difficulty we have as primary colleagues, as Bryony expertly summarised earlier, is that we have to cover so many subject areas that it can be difficult to know how to develop these areas.

Following our discussion on Primary Education Voices, I was impressed not only by Bryony's clear expertise in Primary Science, but also by her knowledge of accessing support and development in all areas of the curriculum for subject knowledge. Whether you are working in the classroom or you have wider areas of leadership that require you to train those who are in classrooms, a strong subject knowledge in the curriculum is important. School leaders will welcome a teacher who wants to develop themselves, so consider the following and choose from Bryony's excellent suggestions on how you will seek that improvement.

Reflecting on the voices of primary education

■ Which subject areas would you consider to be "weak points" in your knowledge?

_____

_____

_____

_____

_____

_____

■ Which development opportunities will you seek in that subject?

_____

_____

_____

_____

_____

_____

■ Which areas are you responsible for and which subject development programmes or awards would support you in your vision for that subject?

_____

_____

_____

_____

_____

_____

6

Using books in the classroom

Simon Smith – @smithsmm
Rich Simpson – @richreadalot

Using books in the curriculum – not just for English – has featured heavily throughout the Primary Education Voices podcast journey. So much so that it demands its own chapter! It is an area that I have gained so much from, being able to speak to these passionate educators who know that using books as a driver for the learning in the classroom and the school is vital. In considering who to ask to contribute to this section, there were a vast number I could have called on, and should there ever be an opportunity to share more, then there would be a large number more.

In this collation, we have two such educators who won't be a surprise for those of you that engage in the Twitter sphere of education (and if you do not, then you must get yourselves on there and connect with these two great advocates for children's books)! Simon Smith will share his knowledge and insights about how using picture books can enhance the quality of learning that takes place in the classroom as well as his top tips on how to use them. Rich Simpson will then share examples of how he uses books as drivers across the school curriculum – going in-depth into a particular example that he has been kind enough to share for us to learn from.

DOI: 10.4324/9781003307150-6

Picture books are not just for little kids: Why picture books should be part of a good primary school curriculum

Simon Smith

"You cannot write for children .... They are much too complicated. You can only write books that are of interest to them."

Maurice Sendak, Author of "Where the Wild Things Are"

I love picture books. I would go as far as to say I am obsessed by them. And because of that – because I use them all the time in my teaching and rave about them in our school – I know something that those schools less keen on picture books do not: they are an absolutely essential tool for developing literacy.

Wonderful, amazing, creative, challenging, funny, heart-breaking, tragic, unbelievable and fabulous picture books. They are not just a vital stepping stone into higher level reading. *They are the missing link.* They can develop in all learners the ability to explore, notice, question, predict, summarise, theorise and analyse.

Picture books are often dismissed as being for younger children. They are not! They are written off as easy. They are not! There are some stunning picture books out there. Many offer us more than they seem to at first. Many require us to bring in our own cultural understanding to truly make meaning of them. People who dismiss them more often than not haven't put the time in to understand and explore them.

Picture books are more than just that they also are a vital part of how we set children free on the journey of reading.

In education, we want, it seems, to be instructed on meaning. Current assessment procedures lead us to this pre-scribed interpretation of meaning, "this tells us this ... this is what this means."

By enforcing meaning and interpretation, we are denying the children one of the fundamental joys of reading: exploring and interpreting for themselves; guided, not told, by the teacher; bringing their own understanding and knowledge to shape the interpretation of the book.

Why is this important? Leland et al. (2005) suggest that "children who experience a critical approach to literacy learn to 'read between the lines' and generate alternative explanations regarding the author's intent. They are encouraged to take an active role in questioning both the texts themselves and the beliefs and personal experiences they bring to them."

Benefits of picture books

By using picture books, we also create, as Martin Galway, English teaching and learning adviser with Herts for Learning, puts it "a swift democracy, a shared world experience that can mitigate/compensate for varying levels of experience of the world."

By reading picture books we are all experiencing for the first time, we can remove barriers to entry. "There is an accessibility to picture books that the written word cannot offer," Matt Tobin.

And picture books allow us all access to explore and interpret. They are routes into inference and deduction and critical thinking. They are an amazing resource to enable children to "make meaning through thinking and discussion" as Mary Roche, a former primary teacher now a lecturer in teacher education, says. She writes wonderfully on this in her book "Developing Children's Critical Thinking through Picture books."

I passionately believe that picture books should form a part of that full reading curriculum. The key bit about picture books is the talk we generate with them, creating time to explore/discuss/challenge our interpretations and helps us understand that there are many ways to interpret a text. The discussion part is one of the key elements in creating enjoyment around books. Finding that there is more than one answer or interpretation can be a profound revelation for children.

As Margaret Meek (1988) says:

Compare the textual variety of children's picture books with that of reading schemes. You will see how the interactions made possible by skilled artists and writers far outweigh what can be learned from books made up by those who offer readers no excitement, no challenge, no real help ... What texts teach is a process of discovery for readers, not a programme of instruction for teachers.

I want our curriculum to do more. A curriculum that gives children the knowledge and then the room to think. A curriculum that encourages children to view the facts through a range of perspectives. The more I think about curriculum, the more I want it to do. I want the young people that leave our school to be questioning, curious and thoughtful. I want them to take evidence and apply their knowledge. We run the risk of overstuffing our curriculum and not really getting to the point of it, a curriculum where a lot is learned but little is signified. A curriculum without soul.

A great curriculum is one that is full of stories. Story in my opinion should run through a curriculum. Curriculum is a narrative, both in its small stories but also in its huge sweeping arcs. Story is threaded through our curriculum, but the curriculum is not completely set in stone. A curriculum requires flexibility to embrace the world around it. History is important not because children know the past but because it truly helps them think about the now.

A curriculum should also be one that asks young people to think deeply about the things they know and apply that knowledge to their understanding. A great curriculum is about perspectives: it is about how we ask children to think about what they know and is about creating a lens to look at what they have learned but also to look at the world around them. Curriculum is not black and white; it is about creating nuance and seeing the stories within the facts. As part of that, we need to see the role reading plays in that, and when we choose books, we need to think hard about why we pick the books we choose. We need to explore our *Purposes for Reading*.

- Read to learn something new
- Read to make us think
- Read to be entertained
- Read to be inspired
- Read to inform
- Read to help us understand others better
- Read to help us understand ourselves

Picture books should completely be part of that range of texts and reading that is offered to the children in our schools.

But let us clarify what I mean by picture books. I am talking about books where the art and the words work together to create meaning so that without either the story is nonsensical.

As people we are fundamentally drawn to story. We remember story, we embrace story. In my opinion, a great school curriculum is one that is infused by story. Curriculum should sit on a bed of stories, both fictional and true. Learning stuff and building knowledge should be a framework for hanging our stories on and a key to helping us understand those stories. Dates, times, events, facts and vocabulary should all be part of helping us understand story.

Fiction and non-fiction picture books should form part of our curriculum offer; picture books can often help us explore complex and challenging ideas.

Moth by Isabel Thomas and Daniel Egneus, for example, takes the Theory of Evolution and succinctly explains it through a story of adaptation and change. *The Journey* by Francesca Sanna is a heart-breaking story of forced immigration due to war and is powerful and poignant. *I Talk like a River* by Jordan Scott and Sydney Smith is a profound exploration of living with a stutter that more clearly shows the perspective better than anything else I have read. *On Wings of Words* by Jennifer Berne and Bruce Steadlander is a stunningly realised picture book biography which gives real insight into the life of Emily Dickenson and casts fresh light on her beautiful poetry. Or *The Invisible* by Tom Percival is a poignant story about poverty and community.

The fact is that best picture books do so much more than tell a story:

1. They elicit emotion (often in my case tears)
2. They confuse and challenge
3. They broach difficult issues in wonderful ways
4. They expect the reader to think
5. They open doors to other cultures
6. They provide leaps of imagination
7. They are wild and playful
8. They are quiet and thoughtful
9. They require the reader to fill in the gaps

So, if you are still with me, then the next question should be OK which books and how should we use them?

I could tell you all day about books, but I would absolutely recommend following Karl Duke on Twitter, who has compiled some utterly amazing lists of picture books linked to curriculum areas.

Here are my top tips.

Firstly, we need to help children look differently at the books, it is not always clear and there is almost always more to it. So here are some key questions:

- Why has the illustrator put that there?
- What do they want us to think at this point?
- How does the word and image work together?

To explore picture books effectively, we need to see the illustrator as an author. The art will often tell us something to the text, it may even contradict the text. Mat Tobin explains very well about codes in picture books, and this has proved to be something extremely useful in helping the children in our school dig deeper into the books meaning.

Using picture books only works if you give children the room to talk and discuss. With that in mind, preparation is key. These questions might help.

- KEY QUESTION 1: What knowledge would help the children explore the book better?
- KEY QUESTION 2: Do you give children room to ask questions about what they are reading?
- KEY QUESTION 3: Do you know the book well enough to dig deeper into it with the children?

The key is not to rush but to explore, to go on a journey through a book with your class. The right book will help pupils think more widely. It will challenge what they are thinking and will help them explore perspectives and viewpoints. So final tips.

1. *Pick your books carefully* There are many wonderful books and is a good starting point for finding titles. Or just go on Twitter, where there are loads of people sharing brilliant books. What you are looking for are books that give you the chance to explore, books that do not give you all the answers.
2. *Develop your understanding of how picture books work* Understanding the picture book codes – position, line, perspective and colour – can change understanding and

interpretation. The codes give children a framework for interpretation and from that they can understand the craft of picture books (Mat Tobin is brilliant on this).

3. *Do not be overly prescriptive with interpretation* Let the children explore. Create the time and space to *TALK* about the books.

4. *If you can get a visualiser, great* It makes exploring easier. To be able to share the close-up detail with the whole class allows children to understand the nuance in the art or to really explore what is there. You can really focus on the detail.

5. *Enjoy them* Picture books have a lot to offer adults, too. Embrace them and sharing picture books will be an absolute joy.

The key to it all is ultimately down to the opportunities we give children to talk about books without that, reading will only be something that children do rather than something that they really want to do.

When I began the journey of stepping into the podcasting world, Simon Smith was a name that rang from the lips of many primary educators. I wanted to produce a podcast that was focused on primary education and that brought to the microphone people who had been an inspiration. They didn't need to have written a book, they didn't need thousands of followers on Twitter – they simply had to have inspired at least one person with an insight or idea into primary education. So, when Simon Smith's name was mentioned by several people before I even began recording my first episode, I knew I needed him on Primary Education Voices. I think Simon also holds the record for the most amount of "name-drops" in recording episodes with others (a person that they mention as a person whom they've learned from).

His passion and knowledge about picture books is legendary. I am confident that if I am crafting a curriculum for a new topic, Simon will either know at least two or three picture books to enhance that topic or be able to point me in the direction of those who will. When I read his submission for this book, I straightaway started to consider which topics I was teaching next half term and how I could fit more stories into them to really enhance the learning experience.

I was grateful for his recommendations on books, people to seek further but also the advice he gives on using picture books. I think that it is very easy as teachers to try and script out exactly what the children should be finding when exploring picture books, but Simon's advice to give children the space and time to explore is wise. Recently, I started using a wordless picture book called "Journey" by Aaron Becker. I followed the advice of Simon, given above, to not be overly prescriptive and to ask questions such as "Why has the illustrator put that there?" What followed was an incredible lesson where the children were noticing details that my year partner and I had missed which embellished the story further. We had been struggling with our particular cohort on writing narratives; they simply didn't have the instinctive flow yet on moving a story forward without clear scaffolded steps. This wordless book was inspirational and helped the class get into the flow of a story without feeling the need to be told how to structure certain parts of the story with their own words. Hopefully, Simon's words guide you to implementing picture books more into your teaching and with more precision on drawing the best creative opportunities out of them.

Reflecting on the voices of primary education

■ Does your school reading offer explore the wide range of purposes for reading?

_____

_____

_____

_____

_____

■ What is your favourite picture book? If you haven't got one, which ones might you try?

_____

_____

_____

_____

_____

> ■ How will you use picture books in your classroom and your
>   school?
>
> _____
>
> _____
>
> _____
>
> _____
>
> _____

Building on a book – Using books as drivers for cross curricular writing

Rich Simpson

In the requirements of the new national curriculum and its knowledge- and fact-based demands, it's easy to treat each subject in isolation, looking only at the skills and progression within it, year on year.

Look at your own school … does each subject have its own leader? Ask yourself, then, how often do these subject leaders sit down and spend planning time with other subjects, looking at how they can be linked and taught together, building on the connections and learning in other areas too?

I've seen some great examples of this. Collaborative cross-curricular teaching, often referred to as "topic" or theme, and when I was fully class-based, I loved nothing more than teaching where things could be linked, cross-referenced, built on and taught together, not jumping from subject to subject in sessions throughout the day. I liked nothing more than when asked what they'd done in a day, a pupil answered "book stuff," not realising they'd covered a plethora of History, Geography, Science, Art and English objectives unwittingly and in detail!

What I'm talking about here isn't anything new … it's referred to as text-drivers, teaching through a text, cross-curricular and many more iterations depending on what schemes you use, CPD you've done or Local Authority you teach in. Loving books, I liked nothing more than finding a text that could be read and enjoyed (Reading for Pleasure, tick) but then also used as the inspiration or model for writing, investigation or linked work in many other subjects, and with the use of so many other texts as well, branching out from it.

I'm sharing here an example of planning created for use with Katherine Rundell's amazing The Explorer book ....

	Cross curricular writing links:
Texts/Key Titles: 'The Explorer' by Katherine Rundell (fiction): 'Survivors', David Long (non-fiction)	SCIENCE: reports on endangered animals, explanations of plant and animal adaptations to environment.
Links to other texts: Shackleton's Journey; Polar Bear Explorer's Club; Jungle Survival Handbook; Botanicum; Historium; Animalium; The Chocolate Tree; a range of History/geographynon-fiction about South America/Mayans	
Outcomes (extended writing opportunities):	Biography of Newton/ Darwin etc
Recounts (newspaper report about disappearance and crash; survivor's recount after rescue)	GEOGRAPHY: description of river environment/ journey/Amazon/ Brazil, explanation of geological processes and activity along a river, recount of a visit
Diaries as a survivor of a disaster - imagined (in role as character from 'Explorer' or real - eg Shackleton)	
NC Reports (about the Amazon: river & rainforest, wildlife endangerment/deforestation etc.)	
Skills linked to curriculum objectives (taken directly from National Curriculum):	HISTORY: Explanations of Mayan life, writing in role, non-chronological report about Mayans, Mayan myths and gods

■ Reading
  ■ continuing to read and discuss an increasingly wide range of fiction
  ■ identifying and discussing themes and conventions in and across a wide range of writing
  ■ making comparisons within and across books
  ■ checking that the book makes sense to them, discussing their understanding and exploring the meaning of words in context
  ■ asking questions to improve their understanding
	ART: biography of Henri Rousseau (related to 'Surprise!' and jungle paintings)
	
	ICT: internet research, Google maps/voyage; internet safety: Tree Octopus report

- drawing inferences such as inferring characters' feelings, thoughts and motives from their actions, and justifying inferences with evidence
- predicting what might happen from details stated and implied
- summarising the main ideas drawn from more than 1 paragraph, identifying key details that support the main ideas
- identifying how language, structure and presentation contribute to meaning
- discuss and evaluate how authors use language, including figurative language, considering the impact on the reader
- distinguish between statements of fact and opinion
- retrieve, record and present information from non-fiction
- participate in discussions about books that are read to them and those they can read for themselves, building on their own and others' ideas and challenging views courteously

PSHE: dealing with difficulties; getting on with others/working as a team; impact of behaviour on others; differences between cultures; awareness of historical behaviours; what to do when things go wrong

- Writing
  - use dictionaries to check the spelling and meaning of words
  - use a thesaurus
  - Identifying the audience for and purpose of the writing, selecting the appropriate form and using other similar writing as models for their own.
  - Noting and developing initial ideas, drawing on reading and research where necessary.
  - using a wide range of devices to build cohesion within and across paragraphs
  - using further organisational and presentational devices to structure text and to guide the reader
  - assessing the effectiveness of their own and others' writing
  - proposing changes to vocabulary, grammar and punctuation to enhance effects and clarify meaning
  - ensuring the consistent and correct use of tense throughout a piece of writing

- ensuring correct subject and verb agreement when using singular and plural, distinguishing between the language of speech and writing and choosing the appropriate register
- proofread for spelling and punctuation errors

- Grammar, Spelling and Punctuation (within writing, and alongside discrete NNS lessons)
  - recognising vocabulary and structures that are appropriate for formal speech and writing, including subjunctive forms
  - using passive verbs to affect the presentation of information in a sentence
  - using expanded noun phrases to convey complicated information concisely
  - using modal verbs or adverbs to indicate degrees of possibility
  - using brackets, dashes or commas to indicate parenthesis
  - using semicolons, colons or dashes to mark boundaries between independent clauses
  - using a colon to introduce a list
  - punctuating bullet points consistently

- Drama, Speaking and Listening
  - listen and respond appropriately to adults and their peers
  - ask relevant questions to extend their understanding and knowledge
  - use relevant strategies to build their vocabulary
  - articulate and justify answers, arguments and opinions
  - participate In discussions, presentations, performances, roleplay/improvisations and debates
  - gain, maintain and monitor the interest of the listener(s)
  - consider and evaluate different viewpoints, attending to and building on the contributions of others

Skill	Task
Identify themes across texts	Book journal/notes; booktalk grids
Retrieve information from NF	Comprehension - Volvo Ocean Race Short write as on-board reporter using picture as prompt Comprehension Qs from Benedict Allen articles
Compare within and across texts	Compare 'The Explorer' with real-life story from 'Survivors'. Table of similarities/differences
Identify language, structure and presentation of text -passive	Annotate a news report for features and discuss language choices and effect. '5 months at sea' story; further stories from 'Survivors'.
■ drawing inferences such as inferring characters' feelings, thoughts and motives from their actions, and justifying inferences with evidence ■ predicting what might happen from details stated and implied	Annotate, discuss and answer SATs and VIPERS questions about selected extracts (from Explorer and other texts: follow up - use texts as models for writing if possible) VIPERS Qs chapter by chapter (take from Literacy Shed website documents)
Choose vocabulary for effect; select appropriate form and style for writing	Make up possible headlines for Explorer story (plane crash) and write a first paragraph of news report. Write a cliff-hanger (in style of blurb on book)

Note and develop ideas; draw on research	Questions to class visitor (adventurer/MP) and research on his website about his trip/job. PSHE
Choose appropriate form for writing; past/present tense use	Write a recount of visit (from e.g. Nick Pointing/outdoor pursuit leader/adventurer?)
How language choices affect readers	Newspaper analysis and discussion (style/content/audience etc.; match headlines to techniques used by writers: pun, rhyme, question, alliteration, shock etc. Write own headline
Identify form and structure of writing	Annotate example of story - use technical language and focus on structure: lead, body, tail etc.
Justify opinions with reference to text (or notes made during a visit)	Comprehension style Qs from Explorer - related to leadership and qualities of characters. Write questions for and take notes during a class visit from expedition leader/visitors.
Plan and edit; retrieve, record and present information from NF	Research Percy Fawcett (explorer - Mayans link) and make notes (biography?) Plan news report - shared writing of 'leads', children to plan 'lead', 'body' and 'tail' of their chosen story.

Plan, write and edit; chose appropriate form for writing	Long writes: ■ News report (Explorer & Tiger escape) ■ Mayans NC report ■ Biography of Mary Anning
Learn a wider range of poetry by heart; compose and perform own compositions	Poem in style of 'The Eagle' using Amazon animal as basis
Look at 'Lost Words' and endangered animals linked to endangered words and text	Plan own poem for an endangered species and illustrate (in style of Lost Words text/art
Identifying the audience for and purpose of the writing, selecting the appropriate form and using other similar writing as models for their own. -verb tense	Diary of Shackleton using 'Ice Trap' picture book as link text (Explorers) across a period of time on his journey
participate in discussions, presentations, performances, roleplay/improvisations and debates	Deforestation/palm oil topic
Identifying the audience for and purpose of the writing, selecting the appropriate form and using other similar writing as models for their own. -modal verbs	Orangutan short movie and comprehension tasks: information sheet/ persuasive letter/ leaflet?
Reading Comprehension SATs practice	Comprehension Ninja Deforestation text
Identifying the audience for and purpose of the writing, selecting the appropriate form and using other similar writing as models for their own. -punctuating bullet points consistently	Instructions for how to catch and cook a tarantula after video clip and extract comparisons. http://www.bbc.co.uk/blogs/food/2011/02/tarantula-kebab-anyone.shtml https://www.youtube.com/watch?v=J5oM3NCf05M

Compare within and across texts (Links to other texts)	See: 'Polar Bear Explorer's club' planning Lost City of Z (extracts) Percy Fawcett picture book (read and discuss)
Identifying the audience for and purpose of the writing, selecting the appropriate form and using other similar writing as models for their own.	Write the next chapter of 'The Explorer' after first encounter on clifftop/at ruins
Identifying the audience for and purpose of the writing, selecting the appropriate form and using other similar writing as models for their own.	Write a Mayan myth style story, using 'The Chocolate Tree' as box-up of structure/model
Plan and edit; retrieve, record and present information from NF	Research Mayan gods and temples, present information found in various forms : infographics, reports, mind maps etc.
Plan and edit; retrieve, record and present information from NF	'Sneaglegator' text (Pie Corbett?) and SATs type questions, annotate for features; write own report about a hybrid creature / Tree Octopus (fake news website - ICT opportunities).

Links to external websites:

https://digital.artsunit.nsw.edu.au/premiers-reading-challenges/author-videos/2019

https://www.worldbookday.com/online-masterclasses/good-thieves-brave-adventures/

'The Explorer' – Katherine Rundell – writing inspired by the text, and cross curricular opportunities, links to other texts

Richard Simpson

When speaking about children's literature and integrating it into the curriculum, Rich is an absolute master. I hope that being able to see an example of his work and how he intricately makes provision for a wide range of skills with one text inspires you to consider how you can use stimuli from children's stories across your curriculum. When I interviewed Rich on the podcast, the wealth of knowledge he had about different texts to use and the way they can link to areas of the curriculum was astounding. As teachers, we are very time-stretched, so reaching out to individuals like Rich can really work wonders for our workload whilst keeping the quality of content and materials we use with the children of a high standard.

I'm sure if (like me) you are inspired by Rich's ideas and want to get some ideas, he would be more than happy to communicate and share his abundance of book learning-related thoughts!

Reflecting on the voices of primary education

■ Thinking about your curriculum, is there an idea which isn't fuelled by a study of a book?

■ What are some places/people/resources you could link up with today to tap into which texts to use for certain areas of the curriculum?

_____

_____

_____

_____

_____

_____

■ How can you develop a love of books and texts in your classroom using the quality of materials suggested above?

_____

_____

_____

_____

_____

_____

Behaviour and pastoral care

Kate Bodle – @katebodle
Penny Whelan – @pennywpennyw

The children whom we teach have had to navigate a world that has gone through some unprecedented times and challenges. In the past few years alone, there have been significant changes to the way people live and many of those changes have had a major impact on the development of children and young people in our classrooms. As such, as primary educators who play a key role in shaping and forming a child's first excursions into learning, we must be aware of what we can do to make these opportunities more accessible to those who have wider educational needs.

To begin with, Kate Bodle (a SEND network lead and Deputy Head) will discuss on the vital role of a pastoral approach in the classroom that can play and provide some practical applications on how teachers can support children who require reasonable adjustments to be able to access mainstream education. Penny Whelan then shares her insights into how children's behaviour in the classroom can very often be a form of communication and what we as the adults in the classroom can do to break the cycle of negativity and support them with the needs that they are trying to convey.

Supporting mental health and pastoral needs

Kate Bodle

Building a strong pastoral culture in school with a focus on well-being seems to me to be one of the most important things we can do as educators. Children who are unhappy

DOI: 10.4324/9781003307150-7

don't learn, so it's a bit of a no-brainer that a focus on supporting mental health is going to lead to better outcomes all around. However, this can seem overwhelming in itself in some settings. I'm lucky enough to work in a small and nurturing school where staff are valued which in turn helps with the culture of strong pastoral care and well-being. What goes around comes around as they say! If you are reading this as a member of senior leadership team (SLT), then start with the staff and the rest should follow!

Sometimes, the needs of our students seem overwhelming and unending. Over the years, I have completed many courses on mental health, trained as an NLP children's coach and worked hard to upskill myself but I believe that the thing that has made the most difference to the lives of the children I teach and their caregivers is to give my time. That isn't always easy in a busy school environment, but it is possible if you believe in its power and the best of all is that it's free!

Setting the ethos which cares about children

Time is a gift in itself, both for you and others. It isn't a magic cure and you won't always know the impact that giving a bit of yourself can have, but I can reassure that with a bit of time and effort, you will be working on the pastoral needs and mental health of others around you without the need for lots of expensive and specific resources. In our school, we do some "big gesture" things – a well-being day in the Autumn term, anti-bullying week, national kindness day, etc., where we explicitly focus on aspects of mental health and wellness but in reality, it's the small things and in particular "talking" that make the difference. Teachers are visible at the beginning and end of the day – the children and parents are greeted at the gate; teachers chat with children when they meet them in corridors and the SLT team knows the names of every child. Parents have direct email access to teachers and vice versa. We encourage parents to tell us the small niggles so that they don't escalate, and we try to be proactive and responsive (and firm where necessary of course as well!).

Celebrating difference is an integral part of what we do. We try to share role models that are neurodiverse as well as those who found things easier at school, so that all children can see that having SEND, for example, will not limit you if you choose to see these differences in a positive light. We send positive postcards or make phone calls to home and have a celebration assembly to celebrate children within school, praising their efforts and contributions, manners and values as much as academic and sporting achievements – and encourage parents to communicate with us about any external celebrations (such as brownies and cub badges, sports teams out of school or baking cupcakes with little support) so that we can also celebrate these as a school community. This helps children feel valued and accepted for a wide range of talents and interests. For an adult in school to pass a child and comment on something they have done sends the message that the child is thought about by adults around them in a positive way, that they are special and that what they do matters to others.

Probably the thing that struck me most when I started at my present school was that the first agenda item at the staff meeting every week was "The Children." A chance to share concerns and worries, to pass on strategies and to support all focused on that child so that everyone who comes in contact with them has the knowledge they need to support them. I think that is incredibly powerful.

However, sometimes children need a bit more support and first of all you need to know who that is and then work out on how to help them. My ideas in the following are nothing new but are based on some knowledge of coaching and counselling strategies. These don't need long training courses or expensive certificates, but you can obviously do those if you want to. Below are some of my day-to-day strategies that work for me and the people in my care to find out who I need to watch out for and to help with the general issues that come up – if you have big concerns about a child, then you must refer them to professional counselling services via Child and Adolescent Mental Health Service (CAMHS) or private practice – your Special Educational Needs and/or Disabilities Coordinator (SENDCo) or Designated Safeguarding Lead (DSL) should be able to advise you.

Strategies for working with children with concerns

I believe my role is not to fix everything for the children but to listen and support them to find their own strategies to cope with the things they face. To empower a child to fix their own problems is to give them a tool they can use throughout life. Often what we want when faced with our own issues as adults is someone to listen, to ask a few pertinent questions to help us think about what we want to achieve and what steps we need to take. Much as it's nice sometimes for someone to tell you what to do, it doesn't actually empower you to solve the problem yourself next time.

So, on a practical level what can we do to support our children? Take time to notice. Look for the child who is behaving a little differently, is withdrawn or whose behaviour has become more challenging. Are you aware of any triggers or issues at home, how is the group dynamic around that child, has that changed?

A simple check-in can work wonders – asking how someone is can tell you a lot even if their answer is "fine" (and always ask again – are you sure you are fine?) if, of course, you are also listening and observing the silent signals. I schedule more formal regular check-ins with all my class using a variety of methods – a simple note exercise – tell me something that you don't think I know about you (initials in the corner) can unearth not only who has a new hamster but also gives a child an opportunity to say, "I'm struggling in maths," "I'm worried about my Grandma" or "I don't feel well today." There are a variety of electronic options out there – such as TEAMS and the reflect app within that which can give children a quick way to record their emotions in a non-judgemental way whenever you want to – additionally it helps with vocabulary around emotions! What you then do with that information is follow-up where necessary. Sometimes we just do a thumbs up or thumbs down exercise. I would advise mixing it up. I had a mood board with post-its children could add on my door for a while – it worked a treat for a few weeks then it didn't. You need to keep ideas fresh; however, the consistency of having some kind of check-in needs to remain.

Children will reach out to you in many ways, but direct talking can be tricky. I don't often have children coming up to me to say that they are feeling down and if they can talk to me. Some braver souls do but most don't. Once I've identified a need, a walk and talk are often the best way to get them to open up as they don't need to look at you and they don't need to feel they are on the spot. If walking and talking in the playground whilst on duty isn't an option, then asking children to come and help you with a job may also give an opportunity for them to open up in a natural way. They may not talk to you initially, but you have given them some time, they have been chosen by you to do something responsible, they may just have seen they can trust you a little more and the time will come when they may feel they can open up. As an adult, you need to be open and available for when that time comes.

When opening up, some children will be able to articulate how they feel and explain the problems they are facing but for many this is really challenging. I have a little set of toys in my room that I use if this is the case. A worry monster provides a safe space for younger children; they can write or draw the problem and feed it to the monster – I then look at it at a later time and decide whether I need to speak to the child again – for some just putting it in there is enough. Sometimes, I get out some Lego and to build a machine to fix the problem, using vocabulary around the building can help them identify what they need to find within themselves to create a solution.

If possible, use little characters or animal toys to enact the problem. It's amazing how a group of Moshi monster toys can be used to explain a playground dynamic (and the choice of characters can be fascinating too!) Again, whilst playing the children aren't having to look directly at you, they are displacing themselves by using the toys and by looking objectively at the unfolding scenario may also be able to start to see their own solutions – you can prompt empathy by asking how each character feels, something they may not have thought about when only considering their own viewpoint. I would recommend looking at the work of Judy Bartowiak if you want to know more about these techniques.

One of the easiest and quickest resources to use can also be a circle of control poster – I keep a batch on my desk to handout, if necessary. I just downloaded them from the

Internet – there are a few around. Often children (and adults) stress and worry about things that are ultimately completely out of their control; readjusting their focus to the things that are within their control can also help find a solution, for example, I can't control what others think about me, but I can control how I react to others is a very useful one. Discussing control is something useful when supporting parents as well.

Anger or emotional management and regulation is another area that as teachers we often need to support children with. There are great resources such as the "Five Point Scale" and books such as "The Volcano in My Tummy" that are worth looking at. I also find that time is again a great resource here – I have a glitter stick or some fiddle-type toys that I give to children who are brought to me to calm down – I hand it over without words, let them watch or play with it and get on with something else until I hear their breathing calm and I feel they could be ready to talk – there is absolutely no point speaking to someone whose mind is full of emotion, they need time to calm down first.

Also remember schools are teams – you don't need to be the only person to support a child. They will often gravitate to the person they find easy to talk to – sometimes lunchtime staff, office staff, etc., who are able to give a little more time and a personal touch. As long as your staff communicate well, you will be supporting others.

Ultimately – you know your children and you know yourself – do what you can, when you can. Trust that you know when to refer on to someone else and be yourself when talking to a child. I often make notes and then ensure anything pertinent is shared with relevant staff or parents, if appropriate. What you do no matter how small can make a huge difference and you already do. Just take care of yourself, and find someone who will give you a bit of their time too.

I learned a lot from Kate about being more reflective as a practitioner about how to support children in a world which is becoming more and more challenging for our young people. When I was a child, when I returned home the world was left outside and the most contact you would have would be a phone call or people physically coming to your door and knocking. Now, more and more of our young people (at younger and younger ages) are interacting virtually with vast numbers of individuals. In a report by Ofcom (2021), it was reported that 30% of children aged between 5 and 7 are actively using social media apps or sites and that 96% use video-sharing platforms. These, whilst under the supervision and guidance of parents, can have great positive potential – however, they can also be damaging when not supported.

As such, as teachers we are being increasingly asked to work with children who have concerns and challenges. Whilst we have pastoral teams to support with this, Kate's advice to teachers is extensive and valuable and I hope you find something in her comments that can be applied directly into your practice to help support young people that you teach or provide for.

Reflecting on the voices of primary education

■ What approaches can you implement to hear children's thoughts more in an encouraging way?

_____

_____

_____

_____

_____

_____

■ Which resources from Kate's suggestions will you look into?

_____

_____

_____

_____

_____

_____

■ Are there any children you work with currently that you know would benefit from any of the suggestions shared above?

_____

_____

_____

_____

_____

_____

References

Ofcom (2021). Children and parents: media use and attitudes report. https://www.ofcom.org.uk/__data/assets/pdf_file/0025/217825/children-and-parents-media-use-and-attitudes-report-2020-21.pdf

Further Reading

A Volcano in My Tummy: Helping Children to Handle Anger: A Resource Book for Parents, Caregivers and Teachers: Amazon.co.uk: Whitehouse, Pudney: 9780865713499: Books
THE INCREDIBLE 5-POINT SCALE – HOME (5pointscale.com)
Starving the Anger Gremlin for Children Aged 5-9: A Cognitive Behavioural Therapy Workbook on Anger Management: 4 (Gremlin and Thief CBT Workbooks): Amazon.co.uk: Kate Collins-Donnelly: 8601417253120: Books (these books have different age ranges and there are others for anxiety, etc., too).
Family therapist, author and trainer | Bucks | Judy Bartkowiak | Burnham

Behaviour and communication

Penny Whelan

Have you had children in your class that you felt had difficult behaviour? I bet you have, and I bet there were times when you knew exactly how to diffuse the situation. But I also bet there have been times when everything you tried didn't work and you had no idea how to help them. When we talk about behaviour, it's tempting to focus on the negative and extreme;

refusal to do work, disruption, aggression and even violence, but there is so much more than the term covers. What about the children who are selective mutes? Those who are so quiet or shy that they never say a word in front of others and never put up their hand? The children who seek reassurance from you throughout the lesson, or those who never ask for help even though they have no idea what you've asked them to do? There are many types of behaviour that can be noted in even a single lesson, and all of it can tell you something about the child, if you take the time to watch, listen and learn.

Everything we say and do is a form of communication. Most of what we actually say isn't even through words but through non-verbal cues such as our expression, gestures and body language. Albert Mehrabian, a body language researcher, broke down the elements of conversation and reached the conclusion that 55% of what we understand comes from the non-verbal cues (body language, gestures, expression, etc.). Thirty-eight per cent was influenced by vocal elements (tone, pitch, etc.) and only 7% of the information we take from a face-to-face conversation with another person comes from the words they use. I'm not saying that no one is listening to what we say, and of course information is transmitted verbally, but what I am saying is that non-verbal information plays a huge role in our communication with other human beings.

So when we are working with children and young people of any age, it's important to understand that they will communicate sometimes without using words but through their expressions, actions and behaviours. From a special educational needs perspective, many of the pupils I work with will be able to tell you far more through their actions than they ever could with words, and as educators we need to be tuned into these subtle (and sometimes not so subtle) clues.

I can't tell you exactly what every child's or young person's behaviour will mean or how you deal with some individual situations. Unfortunately, it's just not that easy. However, if you get to know the pupils in your care and spend time working with them, talking to them and creating that safe space that they so desperately need and want, you stand a much better chance of being able to unpick why they are acting in a particular way.

Is it a special educational need?

Many children and young people who have behavioural difficulties have a special educational need and/or disability, often speech and language difficulties. This means that they have difficulty expressing themselves, their emotions and their needs. When you find it hard to tell people what you want, this can easily lead to feelings of frustration and anger. Imagine how you'd feel if every day you were asked to do work that you found too difficult or that you didn't understand. You'd start to feel that you weren't very clever, that your friends were better than you, more intelligent and you couldn't live up to the expectations of your teachers. You might feel bored or try to cover your confusion by messing around in the classroom, distracting others, trying to copy from them, etc. All of these things would be noticed and seen as negative, probably earning you a consequence. But the next lesson would be the same, and the next, so the problem would never go away. This could escalate into defiant behaviour or refusal to do work. The child might just stop trying altogether. Why bother when you know you can't do it? It creates a sad sense of worthlessness.

All of these are probably behaviours you recognise in different children you've taught at some point. Were they ever assessed for a Special Educational Need? They may already have had a diagnosis, and there will be lots of children you teach who you know have a SEND which helps to explain how they behave and why, but they still need your support. A diagnosis won't make their difficulties go away, but it helps us to understand what they really need to be able to access the curriculum and make the best possible progress. However, even more will go through school without being flagged as potentially having an additional need and this could lead to further problems for them. Behaviours may escalate and then they become a disruption or are labelled as "naughty." It's important to note here that not everyone wants a diagnosis for their children. They don't want them to be "labelled," but they just want them to be understood and supported. Some people use labels to the detriment of the child and parents and young people are well within their rights to refuse assessments if they want to.

The "naughty child"

I have certainly been guilty in the past of falling into the trap of labelling a child as "naughty," when actually it's the behaviour that we need to name and not the child themselves. What we instead need to focus on is teaching them how important it is to make the correct choice and to choose how they respond to certain situations. The word naughty generally means badly behaved, and once labelled as such, it is very difficult for anyone to shake the title and be able to make more appropriate choices. Part of the problem with the word is the fact that it doesn't give the child any information about what they have done. It doesn't explain that the way in which they answered back made us feel frustrated, or when they lashed out at a peer how it hurt and upset their friend and made us feel angry. We need to be much more specific about how we give feedback and information to the children about their behaviour. If you label them as naughty, they'll start to believe they are that and only that, and they will respond accordingly to your expectations.

Giving clear feedback to the children about what they have done will help them to understand what the undesirable behaviour is and help them to choose alternatives next time. It's the difference between giving feedback to the children in Maths about what they did and how they can improve or just putting a cross in red ink in their book. One tells you that you did something wrong, the other explains that although you made the wrong decision, you have an opportunity to put it right and also guides you in how to do that. Not everyone can work out how to put things right by themselves, and children certainly need support to learn that skill. Being a "naughty child" implies there is no other option, when of course we know that everyone can choose to be anything they want.

Is there a past trauma?

When we say trauma, we instantly think of the worst possible cases where a child has suffered abuse or neglect at the hands of someone else, and of course, sadly, there are many occasions where this is true for individuals. However, there may be trauma that has stemmed from bullying, repeated put-downs by peers or family members, or even throwaway comments that someone made about them at some point. How many of us remember something unkind that someone said to us that really affected us? Worse still, do you remember anything a parent or a teacher said to you that made you feel horrible about yourself? Words stick with you and so does the sense of how that person made you feel.

I can't begin to do justice to the topic of trauma-informed teaching, but I can tell you two excellent books that are a must read for all teachers: "Inside I'm Hurting" by Louise Michelle Bombèr and "The Trauma and Attachment Aware Classroom" by Rebecca Brooks. Just consider carefully what might have happened or be happening in the child's personal life and how this is impacting their decisions, behaviour and day-to-day functioning.

What are the first steps to helping a child with challenging or worrying behaviour?

Compassion

Try to think about what might have led to them behaving in the way that they do. Show them that you are genuinely concerned for them and that you want to be supportive. Be present and show them that you care.

Communication

Talk to the child about their behaviour. Communicate clearly with them about what they do and how it makes others feel. Give them the opportunity to talk about how they feel regularly and build good communication and trust between you. They'll feel more comfortable and are more likely to confide in you or start to change their behaviour if they feel they can trust you. Be honest with them too. If you think they need support beyond what you can give, talk to the SENCO or family workers or whoever you need to, but be honest with the child and explain that you will do everything you can to help them but that you might need other people's help too.

Acceptance

Accept that all children will behave and react differently to things. As soon as you start to accept the individual, you'll start to see them more clearly and you'll start to build confidence in them that they didn't know they were capable of. Not only that, but you'll teach them to accept and love themselves, and that is priceless.

What next?

It's up to us! – If you discover something that your pupil needs more support with, it's your duty to do something about it. We have the responsibility as educators to ensure that all children are able to access the full curriculum, and more than that, we want them all to enjoy coming to school and feel that it is a safe environment for them. We are the adults and it's us who have to help them find a way to overcome any difficulties and try to remove any barriers for them.

Talk! – Spend time talking to them, their parents, your colleagues and anyone else you feel needs to be involved. Get them the support they need and fight for it if you have to. Don't give up on them.

Encourage! – Make sure you encourage the child to make the right choices, sensible choices that will help them to overcome barriers and to develop their attitude and willingness to learn. You might have children who are very quiet in class and try to hide away, or even those with selective mutism. The important thing to do is to build their confidence and encourage them to join in and see their contributions as valuable. Don't force them to speak up or draw attention to their shyness, you're likely to drive them further away from you. A lot can be said for quiet and kind encouragement.

Learn! – Find out everything you can about trauma, attachment, special needs, children in care, etc. Whatever it is, whatever the different needs in your class, make up your mind to learn about those needs and experiences so that you are better able to support them. They need you and you need to know what you're doing.

How do we look after our own well-being when dealing with potentially challenging or worrying behaviours?

We're all well-versed in well-being and we are constantly told and encouraged to consider how we look after ourselves, but as educators, we are still prone to ignore that advice. When you're working with children who display complex behaviours, there are usually complex reasons behind them, and those reasons can be difficult for us to process and release at the end of the day. We often spend much of our time over holidays or weekends thinking about the children in our class who we know have a lot going on, and we worry about them. We are emotionally involved because we know our children and care deeply for them all.

There are many different mindfulness and well-being strategies that you can use to help yourself, but my main advice would be to find a way that will help you to consciously switch off from work. Make the decision to leave work at work and to be completely present when you are at home. I'm sure you'll still have some work to do over the weekend, as we all do, but don't let what happens at school consume your free time. Being a teacher is a wonderful and amazing career choice, but it is only a part of who we are. It doesn't define you. You are so much more.

Sources and book recommendations

Is Non-verbal Communication a Numbers Game? Psychology Today. https://www.psychologytoday.com/gb/blog/beyond-words/201109/is-nonverbal-communication-numbers-game
Inside I'm Hurting – Louise Michelle Bombèr
The Trauma and Attachment Aware Classroom – Rebecca Brooks
A Little Guide for Teachers: Teacher Well-being and Self-care – Adrian Bethune
Leaving Work at Work – James Birchenough
Tiny Voices Talk – Toria Bono
The Explosive Child – Ross W Greene

Discussing behaviour as a form of communication has been eye-opening for me. Very much as Penny described, I went for years in my career just thinking that a child who was displaying disruptive behaviours in my classroom was an annoyance to me – that all I had to do was impose a culture of "zero-tolerance" (a term that I cringe at now) and that they would fall into line. Once that was accomplished we could all get to the end of the school year, part ways and not have to worry about it again.

I really am ashamed of this approach now. I was not looking at the child as a person that would then go on and have to work through the challenges and anxieties that they were going through and I had not given the support for them to work through these things. Penny had some fantastic insights into this area as I was discussing it on Twitter and I felt that she needed to be able to have the platform to share them. I hope that her insights and resources that she cites support you in your journey of supporting children with their challenges and that you begin to see behaviour as a form of communication. If you really listen, you may hear a number of enlightening things that you can do to help them!

Reflecting on the voices of primary education

■ Can you think of any children or young people that may have been displaying behaviour as a form of communication?

_____

_____

_____

_____

_____

■ Which resources from Penny's suggestions will you look into?

_____

_____

_____

_____

_____

- What can you implement from this entire chapter to help you find the headspace to give time and encouragement for children to share their communication more appropriately?

_____

_____

_____

_____

_____

_____

8

Diversity and representation

Kyrstie Stubbs – @kyrstiestubbs
*Kyrome Adams – @MrKAdams_*

In an ever-changing world, educating our children in primary education to be supportive and inclusive world citizens is an often-mentioned priority in developing the whole child. As more interconnectivity reaches across the globe, we are becoming acquainted with further diversity that enriches our lives. The two contributors to this section were interviewed on the podcast and their insights into integrating further representation of all manner of sociocultural issues were powerful. I was keen to have them expound further on these insights in this book.

First, Kyrstie Stubbs (known as the Tattooed Headteacher) shares her school's journey into widening the representation in their curriculum and how they have helped their children feel "seen" in so many ways. She will also refer to the nine protected characteristics that provide us with a useful frame of understanding how we need to diversify our curriculum. Then, Kyrome Adams will share his thoughts on how all educators can "inclusify" their curriculum by giving a variety of examples of individuals who would be key to study in our current National Curriculum.

A children's curriculum

Kyrstie Stubbs

Over the past few years, a lot has been discussed around curriculum development – experts and research all vying for attention and if we were to believe everything we heard or

DOI: 10.4324/9781003307150-8

read then we could never design one that met all of the criteria. What we need to do as leaders is to think about the right curriculum for OUR children and OUR community. For me, curriculum design should be about the children and their needs. If children can't see a point to what they are learning, then they are less likely to engage.

We can argue about how to make learning "real" but the most important factor for me is that for a curriculum to be "real" for the children, this surely means that they are visible in it.

When I started unpicking our curriculum around six years ago, it became very clear to me that for our community of pupils, there was little they could latch onto in terms of their own experiences and many of them were not represented at all.

In fact, if you weren't white, heterosexual, of British decent, and middle class, then there was little you could relate to. A lot of history, for example, was missing or was told from a single perspective or lens – this didn't sit right with me and my team.

When Kyrstie shared this insight in our Primary Education Voices interview, I was impressed with the self-reflection that had occurred here. The quality of representation in our curriculums is something that is beginning to be scrutinised more as schools have implemented what can be considered to be very one-dimensional National Curriculum at face value. However, it is great educators like Kyrstie who can take those objectives and ensure that they help all children in their classes feel seen whilst still covering all the objectives they need to.

What Kyrstie describes here was not unnoticed in the Primary Education world at large. In fact, the diversity found in children's literature was found to be lacking as late as five years ago. A report by the Centre for Literacy in Primary Education (CLPE) called the Reflecting Realities report (CLPE, 2018) found some troubling statistics about all children's literature published in 2017. It stated:

- There were 9115 children's books published in the UK in 2017. Of these, only 391 featured Black, Asian or Minority Ethnic characters (4%)
- Only 1% of the children's books published in the UK in 2017 had a Black, Asian or Minority Ethnic main character
- Over half the fiction books with Black, Asian or Minority Ethnic characters were defined as "contemporary realism" (books set in modern-day landscapes/contexts)

- 10% of books with Black, Asian or Minority Ethnic characters contained "social justice" issues
- Only one book featuring a Black, Asian or Minority Ethnic character was defined as "comedy"
- 26% of the non-fiction submissions were aimed at an "Early Years" audience

If the texts available for teachers to use had such a small proportion that helped all ethnic backgrounds be seen in the written materials that children are reading, then this highlights even further the important task that Kyrstie highlighted that her school had to overcome.

We set about thinking how we could make the curriculum as relevant as we could without putting ourselves in a position where we weren't able to demonstrate we were teaching the "National Curriculum."

We started by looking at the texts we used as our quality texts for English and found out that the majority were written by white authors and the majority had white characters as well and were generally centred around the nuclear family. There are so many wonderful books out there written by diverse authors, with a diverse range of characters and situations. This helped us to improve the range of books we used.

The problem extended to the books we offered to children in both our main library and in classrooms. This took longer due to the investment needed, but we managed over the course of three years to completely overhaul our stocks and therefore the reading diet for our children became much richer and more relevant. The mantra "you can't be what you can't see" is one that I firmly believe in and this is not limited to colour or sexuality but including neuro-diverse characters and authors and those with both hidden and visible disabilities.

Kyrstie notes here that whilst their school library reflected the "reality" in the Reflecting Realities report, there was still quality out there that could help to diversify the texts that her school used. Since the report was published in 2018, there has been some shift. In the fourth version of the report published in 2021 that analysed children's literature published in 2020, CLPE found:

- A positive increase in children's books featuring a minority ethnic character from 10% in 2019 to 15% in 2020 and up significantly from the 4% reported in the inaugural report in 2017
- Increase in representation in picture books and non-fiction – representation in fiction books remains the same
- The Reflecting Realities reports have inspired a number of initiatives from a variety of organisations, implying positive change in the industry

Clearly there is change happening, and it is becoming more and more possible for teachers and leaders to reflect on the representation in their school's book resources and ensure that variety is shown – not just in the ethnicity of the characters but in other sociocultural areas also.

One of the most useful activities we did as a team was to map exactly which countries in the world we actually taught children about as part of our geography curriculum. In a school with pupils of many different nationalities, we were teaching them about such a small percentage of the world and, even then, not the countries that represented them or their background and culture. Even where we were teaching about countries with some relevance for our children we felt we were teaching a single narrative, possibly even strengthening stereotypes rather than challenging them.

We set about changing this by going through our history and geography curriculums as a starting point. It meant a lot of research to find out accurate facts and this alone strengthened our desire to ensure the curriculum was changed – if we had been taught ourselves when we were at school "real" history rather than a one-sided account, then we would not have had to do as much research surely. It certainly started with us asking more questions than finding answers!

There was also a gap in educating children about what equity is and why it is so important that we all work towards a better understanding. Teaching children about representation and equity in primary schools is vital as a foundation on which they can further develop. It is not right for educators to pick and choose among the nine protected characteristics we teach – morally we should address bias and stereotypes

across all of the nine characteristics and dismantling racism, homophobia and all discrimination from a very young age.

I think that this is a powerful and important point made here by Kyrstie. When speaking of diversity and representation in the curriculum, we may only be thinking of one or two of the sociocultural issues that we could be addressing. Kyrstie mentions the following nine protected characteristics defined under the Equality Act in 2010:

- age
- disability
- gender reassignment
- marriage and civil partnership
- pregnancy and maternity
- race
- religion or belief
- sex
- sexual orientation

As Kyrstie stated, it is important for all primary educators to consider how these will be addressed in their classes. Of course there are important ways to approach them in an age-appropriate manner, but I believe that all nine characteristics can be addressed in some way in different phases of primary education.

In the Early Years Foundation Stage, these discussions may be focused through stories that represent all types of family structures, which introduce children who are disabled in some way, or through talking about relationships and how to build healthy, lasting relationships with others who may have some differences to them. When you start to reflect on examples like these, it becomes clear how the groundwork can be laid for future discussion of all of these characteristics.

It can be easy to persuade yourself as a leader that it can be "left" until children go to secondary school but in my view, it is too late by this point to really influence children's views and therefore attempt to change the current narrative of bias. The sheer fact that teaching or tackling some of these issues will be difficult is the absolute reason that we MUST, as educators, start to really address them as soon as children enter the education system.

I often have discussions with leaders who tell me that they don't need to teach aspects of diversity or representation as their communities are all white, for example. NO, NO and NO! In fact, in these communities, I think it is possibly even more important that we teach children about difference and how to celebrate it.

We need to be using the cultural heritage in our communities to support children's learning and where this is limited to be exposing children to other cultures they have less lived experience with if we are truly going to start educating children for the world in which we live in.

I have a real passion for teaching children the "truth" about our past so that we can all learn from it – in the words of Nelson Mandela, "education is the most powerful weapon which you can use to change the world."

Having Kyrstie on the podcast was fantastic because she spoke powerfully about how we can shift the paradigm in a number of areas, including her Extended Curriculum which gives time in the week for every child in her school to experience skills such as crafting, den building and all manner of activities that seek to build the whole child, whilst still covering all objectives in the National Curriculum (if you're interested in that, you'll have to go and listen)!

However, her discussion about representation and her own personal experience with this was incredible and so I had to ask her to include some wider thoughts into this. All schools will be at different stages with this. Some may not have considered this at all. Some may have identified a couple of the nine protected characteristics and have started to address them, such as religion or belief and race but not others. A few may be well on the way with all nine. Wherever your class or school is, it is worth reflecting on what the next steps are to go further along this important and inclusive journey. Look for the next small step, review what Kyrstie has said here and start to put a plan in place. Anything to raise awareness on these issues is better than looking at the enormity of it and doing nothing.

References

CLPE (2018). Reflecting Realities – Survey of Ethnic Representation within UK Children's Literature.

CLPE (2021). Reflecting Realities – Survey of Ethnic Representation within UK Children's Literature.

Reflecting on the voices of primary education

■ How inclusive is the curriculum in your school?

_____

_____

_____

_____

_____

_____

■ What are the next steps to develop the characteristics selected above?

_____

_____

_____

_____

_____

_____

■ Which of the nine protected characteristics could be developed further in your curriculum?

_____

_____

_____

_____

_____

_____

Inclusify your curriculum

Kyrome Adams

As educators, we can change the world. Big statement, I know. But it's true.

There is so much conflict and hatred. My thought is: Where does that discrimination come from? Children aren't born racist, ableist or homophobic. It is learned behaviour.

Introducing children to people who are different to them from a young age WILL make a *world* of difference. But how should we do this?

First, look at your curriculum. Is it well thought out? Are your children *seen* (an emphasis on the word "seen"!) in your curriculum? When something is relatable, you are naturally more invested. I wasn't seen in my school learning. The only reference I had to someone who looked like me was in history learning about slaves. On a reflection, as an adult, I just know how valued I would have felt if I learned about people – other than slaves – that looked like me. It may sound juvenile, but I HATED dress-up days such as World Book Day and topic days etc. as I felt I could never fully be that character or historical figure due to my skin colour. Now, I am not blaming my schools (I had a great primary and secondary experience) but the curriculum was delivered through a white lens.

Where was the teaching of Septimius Severus, a Roman leader, who was much more successful than Julius Caesar; John Blank from the Tudor period who rallied for more wages and won; Ira Aldridge, a very famous actor in Victorian Britain; Mary Seacole and Walter Tull – the list goes on. When I discovered Walter Tull, my mind was blown; a black soldier in WW1, what?! I'd only seen pictures of white soldiers. My point is: when I have faced racism and have been called a slave several times, IMAGINE if I could have rebutted with: black people weren't just slaves; we were leaders of empires; we nursed people back to life; we were commissioned officers!

It is crucial, vital and paramount (insert all the other synonyms!) that the rising generation receive a curriculum that is full of colour. A diverse curriculum. We are a huge melting pot, and we will come across individuals who are different from us. Visibility leads to understanding and understanding leads to acceptance. If this is done right, this would lead to creating understanding and compassionate individuals, and who doesn't want that?

As teachers, we are busy but please don't just continue to teach what you were taught, inclusify your curriculum. Inclusify is not a real world but I like how it sounds.

Here is a starting point. This is NOT at all an exhaustive list, but it should get you started.

Main teaching periods covered in schools.

Black influential figures:

TIME PERIOD	FIGURE (WHO)	IMAGE(S)
Romans 43 AD–410 AD	*Septimius Severus* was an African Emperor who was born in North Africa in AD 145. He came to Britain in AD 208. The governor explained that they were being attacked from the North, so he built the walls of Roman London. In 193 AD, he became the sole emperor of the Roman Empire.	Statue outside of the British Museum  https://www. britishmuseum. org/collection/ object/G_1802-0710-2
Tudors 1484–1603	*John Blank* (blank because he was black) was a trumpeter. He is also the first black person to have a picture on record. He became popular as he rallied for more wages and won, so he was paid equal to white counterparts. He wasn't a "slave" – in images (tapestry), he is seen to be wearing rings, so it can be inferred that he had some wealth.	 https://en.wikipedia. org/wiki/John_Blanke *(Continued)*

TIME PERIOD	FIGURE (WHO)	IMAGE(S)
Victorians 1837–1901	*Ira Aldridge* was a well-known actor in Victorian Britain.	 https://commons. wikimedia.org/wiki/ File:Portrait_of_Ira_ Aldridge,_by_Taras_ Shevchenko_(1858).jpg
	Mary Seacole (Mother Seacole) had a MASSIVE contribution in the Crimean War at the age of 50. She also opened the British Hotel which had a restaurant, shops and a clinic.	 https://commons. wikimedia.org/wiki/ File:Portrait_of_Ira_ Aldridge,_by_Taras_ Shevchenko_(1858).jpg
Great War 1914–1918	*Walter Tull* was a professional footballer who signed Tottenham at the age of 21 for £10. He then became the first black commissioned officer in the army. Unfortunately, he died at the age of 29 while fighting in the Somme.	https://www. bbc.co.uk/sport/ football/43504448

Asian influential figures:

TIME PERIOD	FIGURE (WHO)	IMAGE(S)
Great War 1914–1918	*Princess Sophia Duleep Singh* is best known as a suffragette and campaigner for women's rights. Daughter of deposed Maharaja Duleep Singh and goddaughter of Queen Victoria. She used her fame, position and tenacity in the fight for gender equality in the early 20th century.	 https://essexcdp.com/ event/fnap-princess- sophia-exhibition/
World War II 1 September 1939–2 September 1945	*Noor-un-Nisa Inayat Khan*, GC, also known as Nora Inayat-Khan and Nora Baker, was a British resistance agent in France in World War II who served as the Special Operations Executive (basically, a spy in the war).	 https://www. thoughtco.com/ noor-inayat-khan- biography-4582812
17 March 1962–1 February 2003	*Kalpana Chawla* was an American astronaut and engineer. She was the first woman of Indian descent to go to space.	 https://en.wikipedia.org/ wiki/Kalpana_Chawla *(Continued)*

TIME PERIOD	FIGURE (WHO)	IMAGE(S)
23 June 1936–1 September 2002	*Yuji Ichioka* was an American historian and civil rights activist.	https://alchetron.com/ Yuji-Ichioka

BOOKS, BOOKS, BOOKS!

We can learn so much through literature. It is empowering in the way it transmits discourse and ideology. It's so important that our children can see themselves reflecting on what they read. There are so many brilliant books out there. Start slow and over time your bookshelf should represent a wide demographic of people: those in wheelchairs, those who have hearing aids and those who wear religious dress.

Cheeky plug: myself, Jasmine Newton and Toni Ansell wrote a book called *My Daddy Changed the World* to help aid conversations regarding discrimination. This book is a social story about the discrimination a black person may face. It is written for children to help them understand such injustices and to aid important conversations through pictures.

One of my favourite books to use is *The Proudest Blue* by Ibtihaj Muhammad and S.K. Ali. The book illustrates the beauty of the hijab and how togetherness and being proud of who you are can help overcome hurtful words. In my current school, many children and parents wear a hijab and by sharing this book, it has made children who were reluctant to wear their traditional dress proud to do so.

Another favourite of mine is *My Hair* by Hannah Lee and Allen Fatimaharan. This book is an ode to the beauty of a black person's hair and all the wonderful forms it can take. Similarly, to the Proudest Blue, it is about being proud of who you are and comfortable with the skin you're in. Such an important conversation to have and the one I've had with my nieces. Representation matters.

Ultimately, having a diverse range of books and other resources that represent children, where they can see themselves portrayed in many different ways, will help them grow in confidence and positively view their place in society.

Quick fire tips and tricks:

- When you insert an image on your board, are the pictures representative? Twinkl does a great job of this. Children in hijabs, children of different weights, children with acne. Normalise it.

- Experiences: expose children to a wide range of people. Reach out to your local community and get people to share their life. Celebrate each other. We can learn a lot!

- Lunch time: serve a variety of cuisine every day and NOT JUST on themed days because to some children that "themed lunch" is their norm.

- Resources: do the dolls in continuous provision or other toys in your school have a range of skin colours, hair types etc.?

To conclude, what does an inclusive curriculum mean to me? It's a chance to burst that ecosphere to allow harmony among all.

Honestly, I could have asked Kyrome to delve deeper into his submission on a number of areas we discussed in his Primary Education Voices episode – he is a great educator. However, I felt inspired by the conversation we had on this very important topic. Many schools are reviewing their curriculum at this time and it is the perfect time for them to identify how they can ensure the children in their school are truly seen in their curriculum.

When reading his own experience growing up in an education system that failed him as a young child in helping him feel recognised as the individual he is, I felt the need to do better. Unless the National Curriculum is developed to specify this, it falls to us as teachers to include curriculum content in what we deliver to help our schools address this important issue.

Unfortunately, what we include or what you should seek for is a little trickier because your children's demographics will be different from the ones in my school and again different from Kyrome's. However, here he gives us some great starting points and the reason why this is an area worth investing some time in. Start small if you need to, identify some figures you can integrate into your curriculum, connect with great people like Kyrome and others he mentions so they can support you if you feel you need pointing in the right direction.

Reflecting on the voices of primary education

- What are the demographics of your classroom - are they all represented in your curriculum?

_____

_____

_____

_____

_____

_____

■ Which historical figures would fit into your curriculum to inclusify your curriculum?

_____

_____

_____

_____

_____

_____

■ What resources are you going to seek out to support this inclusifying, including books?

_____

_____

_____

_____

_____

_____

Using technology in the classroom

Allen Tsui – @TsuiAllen
Matt Roberts – @Mroberts90Matt

We are living in a 21st-century world, and yet very often if you were to look into the average primary classroom, you would think that not much has changed. Aside from the interactive whiteboard screen, which is very often used as a glorified projector, you would be forgiven for thinking that we had been transported back in time decades! Technology can play an integral part in the teaching and learning that take place in our primary classrooms. This should never be done to the detriment of the learning as a gimmick but rather enhance the types of activities we can ask the children to complete.

To help with this, we hear first from Allen Tsui who is an absolute expert in the area of Computing. He shares his experience into how the Computing curriculum, which so often worries primary teachers who have to teach it, can be broken down and taught well in every classroom. I will then share my insights into how technology can, and should, be integrated across the curriculum. This approach will not only open up more time for other content that we need to teach but can provide a greater quality of tasks to engage with across the curriculum as well.

Let's talk IT out …

Allen Tsui

The sad loss of the family pet Syrian hamster, Cookie, in early March 2022 reminded me that my family adopted her on St George's Day 2020 when Britain had been "living" a month

DOI: 10.4324/9781003307150-9

into the measures that had been put in place to combat COVID-19. It was during this time too that I had been curating my existence on Twitter to the point that it attracted @ Mroberts90Matt to invite me to hold the honour of being one of the first guests for the Primary Education Voices podcast series.

Professionally, I had a slow burn completing my post-qualification year and only managed to complete what was then known as Newly Qualified Teacher in March 2016. I was offered the role to lead Computing at the amazing schools I work for in the Summer of 2020.

Being one of the vanguard voices for the Primary Education Voices podcast has allowed me time too to look back over the start of my time as a specialist teacher of Computing. The schools I work for have departed from the path that many Primaries have by following a more Secondary model with subject specialists in Art, Drama, Music and PE as well as Computing teaching across the whole school. Whilst such an approach offers many advantages and benefits, I am mindful of the fact that my immediate colleagues might become "de-skilled" in these subject fields, so I try to secure some succession planning by making all of my lesson planning and learning resources I create as openly accessible as possible.

I would say that for those colleagues in the wider teaching community who might be daunted by the prospect of having to teach technology or use technology to support their teaching, there really is no need to be. With the advent of touch screen technology and "always on" devices, software which operates with their in-built suggestions and learners living in a multimedia-enriched world where technology is ubiquitous, teaching Computing has become no different to Maths or English in terms of its overall pedagogical approach. This may be unfounded personal conjecture and suggested by someone with some subject knowledge. Again, drawing from my time in the Civil Service when I was responsible for implementing a more market-driven path to managing infrastructure projects for the Department I was working for, we had a phrase called the "intelligent client." This meant not needing to be an expert but knowing what questions to ask and whom to ask. Social media has made it possible for the importance of subject knowledge to slightly diminish, especially for Primary practitioners when being classroom-based means having to supposedly be "expert" in every subject. The Computing at Schools Network (Twitter: @CompAtSch) and the National Centre for Computing Education (Twitter: @WeAreComputing) have been my go-to cornerstones since 2016 and 2018, respectively. On personal level, teaching technology and teaching more generally is about being open to learning new ideas and sharing that experience with the families we, as teachers, get to work with. It would be fantastic too for those who have more or greater subject expertise in whatever field to inspire and encourage others by simply remembering to regularly ask our professional peers "what would you like to learn today?" For those schools that do not have the benefit of a technical support partnership to ensure that the technology and audio-visual learning aids are in good working order, it is about always having an "unplugged" back up plan and knowing whom to ask for help at the next earliest available opportunity. Even for those who might be more comfortable with using technology, there will be the unpredictability of when the technology will fail and using such times to teach or demonstrate values such as resilience, adaptability and openness.

Computing into a curriculum

So what do I make teaching Computing look like? My starting point is actually thinking about what @CompAtSch describes as "learner endpoints." Those who have been working in schools for some time might recognise these as "I can" statements based on this awful phrase of "end of Year Age Related Expectations." I really don't like the phrase because linking learning to this chronological construct is both artificial and limits learning. In the time I have been teaching, it has been a privilege and honour working with the families I have whose learning needs have ranged from needing significant support to even access the curriculum to those Year 6 learners who seemingly effortlessly achieved maximum points at the end of Key Stage statutory tests. What I have done therefore is taken a part of the Computing curriculum and listed all of the learning end-points on a single document like this:

Programming targets from the Primary National Curriculum for schools in England since 2014

Year 1	Year 2	Year 3	Year 4	Year 5	Year 6
Give instructions to my friend and follow their instructions to move around.	Give instructions to my friend using forward, backward and turn and physically follow instructions.	Break an open ended problem up into smaller parts.	Use logical thinking to solve an open ended problem by breaking it up into smaller parts.	Decompose a problem into smaller parts to design an algorithm for a specific outcome and use this to write a program.	Deconstruct a problem into smaller parts, recognising similarities to solutions used before.
Describe what happens when I press buttons on a robot.	Tell the order I need to do things to make something happen and talk about this as an algorithm.	Put programming commands into a sequence to achieve a specific outcome.	Use and efficient procedure to simplify a program.	Refine a procedure using repeat commands to improve a program.	Explain and program each of the steps in my algorithm.
Press buttons in the correct order to make a robot do what I want.	Program a robot or software to do a particular task.	Keep testing my program and recognise when I need to debug it.	Know to keep testing a program while putting it together.	Use variables to increase programming possibilities.	Evaluate the effectiveness and efficiency of my algorithm while continually testing the programming of the algorithm.
Describe what actions I will need to do to make something happen and begin to use the word algorithm.	Look at my friend's program and say what will happen.	Use repeat commands.	Recognise that an algorithm will help sequence more complex programs.	Change an input to a program to achieve a different output.	Recognise when using a variable is needed to achieve a required output.
Begin to predict what will happen for a short sequence of instructions.	Use programming software to make objects move.	Describe the algorithm needed for a simple task.	Use a variety of tools to create a program.	Use 'if' and 'then' commands to select an action.	Use a variable and operators to stop a program.
Begin to use software or apps to create movement and patterns on a screen.	Watch a program execute and spot where it goes wrong so that I can debug it.	Detect a problem in an algorithm which could result in unsuccessful programming.	Recognise that algorithms will help in other learning such as Maths, Science as well as Design & Technology.	Use logical reasoning to detect and debug mistakes in a program.	Use different inputs (including sensors); to control a device or onscreen action and predict what will happen.
Use the word debug when I correct mistakes when I program.			Use a sensor to detect a change which can select an action within my program.	Use logical thinking, imagination and creativity to extend a program.	Use logical reasoning to detect and correct errors in algorithms and programs.
				Talk about how a computer model can provide information about a physical system.	

With this structure at the forefront of everybody's minds means that learners can use a learning journey metaphor, travel along a very personalised path at their own pace or speed. While at face value such an approach might be seen by some as being a little slow, what it offers is the ability for the one or two children in every class I have taught in the time I have been working in schools to accelerate ahead. The advantage of being a specialist subject teacher with Secondary experience to pre-University level means that I have sight of where the learning journey needs to be at the end of every Key Stage – not just for Primary. So if there are children who are chronologically in KS2 but able to access the KS3 curriculum, I can, will and do teach that. By way of specific example, there will be children in KS2 who are more than capable of learning to code in a text-based language such as Python using an emulator web-site along with highly scaffolded programming examples to follow.

For those children who are less advanced, with Computing being such a practical subject, it is possible to identify a set of skills to form the minimum standards which must be achieved for that Year group. This is achieved by breaking down each of the targets into sets of skills. Sticking with the programming example, specifically for Year 5, learners must be able to:

Decompose a problem into smaller parts to design an algorithm for a specific outcome and use this to write a program.

Delving into a computing scheme

In planning a lesson or sequence of teaching to achieve this, the big inquiry-based learning question I would set for my Year 5 classes to start the sequence off is to ask "how can I improve the program I am writing?" This big question, inquiry-based approach means taking learners systematically through a programming project such as creating an animation or game so that they focus on their computer programming skills. Within the programming project, there will then be scope to break the project or problem down into smaller parts. The algorithmic design allows learners to describe in a sequence of steps how they expect their program to work or what happens in their program. Here's a simple example:

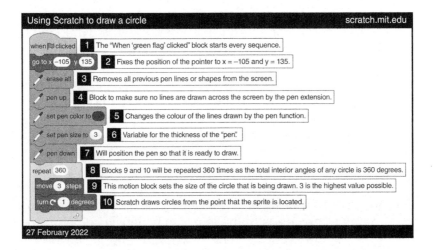

Using Scratch to draw a circle — scratch.mit.edu

1. The "When 'green flag' clicked" block starts every sequence.
2. Fixes the position of the pointer to x = –105 and y = 135.
3. Removes all previous pen lines or shapes from the screen.
4. Block to make sure no lines are drawn across the screen by the pen extension.
5. Changes the colour of the lines drawn by the pen function.
6. Variable for the thickness of the "pen".
7. Will position the pen so that it is ready to draw.
8. Blocks 9 and 10 will be repeated 360 times as the total interior angles of any circle is 360 degrees.
9. This motion block sets the size of the circle that is being drawn. 3 is the highest value possible.
10. Scratch draws circles from the point that the sprite is located.

27 February 2022

In the image, the numbered blocks to the right of the Scratch blocks form the algorithm which has been written as instructions that others should be able to read and understand.

For those reading this and thinking there are some parts of this lesson planning idea which requires a technical understanding, especially when teaching coding or programming, there are, at the time of writing, many organisations that provide training support either a small cost or no cost to up-skill those who feel less technically confident. Platforms like Scratch also have a wealth of enthusiasts who have uploaded "how to" videos on video-sharing websites as well as allowing their Scratch projects to be "remixed" – so using other people's project examples as a starting point. At the time of writing (Spring 2022), Barefoot Computing and Code Club are also fantastic, free-to-access websites with project ideas for teaching computer programming suitable for KS1 and KS2.

In terms of knowing what to teach and when, again there are a wide variety of Schemes of Work available to download from the World Wide Web. Some will charge a subscription for doing so. Others may be included within a membership fee to access a range of resources they produce or publish. Learning platforms such as Purple Mash produce Scheme of Works which are directly linked to the use of their platform. The National Centre of Computing Education (NCCE), which was a consortium formed by the National STEM Learning Centre, Raspberry Pi Foundation and the BCS, Chartered Institute for IT which received £84 million in 2018 from the Department for Education to run a three-year programme of professional support for teachers, has also produce teaching resources which are (currently, Spring 2022) available to freely access. As a personal observation, all of these Schemes of Work are very well structured and provide good coverage of the National Curriculum's statutory expectations. However, they do, without exception, need to be adapted to suit personal teaching styles as well as meeting the needs of the learners which will differ from class to class and year to year. It would therefore be best to try to secure access to a range of Schemes of Work or teaching resource titles to have maximum flexibility in choosing the most appropriate sequence of lessons to teach bearing in mind the needs of the learners and the equipment or resources available in school. There is no point, for example, focusing on keyboard skills when the only devices available are tablets.

Assessing and evaluating an effective computing curriculum

For those who have subject leadership responsibilities, senior leaders will frequently remind us that we are accountable at curriculum level for what is taught. From my own experience, what I have found useful is drawing on the expertise of the Computing at School Network that in 2013 produced a report entitled "Computing in the national curriculum". In this report, they proposed segmenting Computing into three broad fields of study – Computer Science, Digital

Literacy and Information Technology or as I have rebranded IT (quite literally) into Computational Thinking. Soon after the reorganised National Curriculum had begun to be taught in schools, the Royal Society published its own evaluation of how Computing was being taught in schools. Their 2017 report, "After the reboot: computing education in UK schools" identified a deficit in the coverage of how computer-based systems facilitating mass data collection dominate our everyday lives, so advocated Data Handling or Information Science to be a stand-alone component from Digital Literacy or Information Technology. Such an approach would not only enable learning about how data is used, stored and shared but also encourage philosophical debate (Philosophy for Children or "P4C") about ethical and moral implications of such technologies. It was also around this time that the UK Council for Child Internet Safety (that since July 2018 became the UK Council for Internet Safety which is a Non-Departmental Public Body comprising representatives from the Department for Culture Media and Sport and Home Office working with the Department of Education) published its first "Education for a Connected World" framework to address rising concerns over the safe use of computers as communications devices as well as concerns around how easily accessible inappropriate content was available on the World Wide Web.

Where assessment is concerned, the schools I work for have since September 2021 decided to adopt a very highly structured approach. The expectation that has been set is for all subjects to have a written outcome which focuses on knowledge acquisition, the skill being taught and learners being able to demonstrate application of the skill. While such an approach may deeply divide opinion, focusing on a written outcome is no bad thing, especially if it supports the school's reading and writing targets. Such an approach also enables subject leaders to evaluate the impact on learning and see a clear pathway of progress. Furthermore, learners are encouraged to reflect on their habits of effective learning which I have adapted to focus on positive attributes or values of excellence in Computing or Computer Science.

#CASchatWoTD with @TsuiAllen	
Qualities of Computer Scientists Computer Science is about always being...	
creative	as all digital content is. From creating an account to log-in or sign-in to a secure platform to all data types (text, images, sound files and video).
link makers	by applying computational thinking to every task and project.
solution finders	through "thinkering".
knowledge builders	by up-levelling or up-cycling the ideas of others.
technologically tenacious	through resilience and perseverance.
determined	to secure an outcome.
focused	on learning new skills and applying the knowledge from those new skills.
collaborative	and proud to share.
discoverers	by pushing boundaries of what is currently possible.
11 March 2022	Colour swatch created from http://paletton.com/

Since becoming subject lead for Computing, one of the aspects indirectly related to the role I've been positively astonished by is how active the network of teachers and those associated with schools are in making use of social media. Through my sequence of digital citizenship lessons, I am acutely aware that social media platforms have many pitfalls which in our roles as teachers we are expected to warn young learners about. While every social media platform will have its dark corners, the network of teachers who either specialise in Computing or have a keen interest in the subject is really active, very friendly, knowledgeable and eager to support anybody who wants to know more about teaching-specific topics or improving their subject knowledge.

In the interests of transparency and accountability, all of the resources I create or have collected can be accessed via the Wakelet collection (https://wakelet.com/@tsuiallen) I started at the end of 2020.

Allen and I were able to meet for a Primary Education Voices podcast very early on in my journey and he was so gracious. I vividly remember rushing back from the hospital bedside of my son who had recently been diagnosed with leukaemia and running late, but Allen was so helpful with adjusting our time to meet and I was then treated to an absolute masterclass of specific resources that he would recommend teachers get involved in to enhance the Computing curriculum in their class and school.

As such, when the thought of this book began to germinate, I knew that I would need to have Allen on board to help give practical advice and guidance on driving forward an effective Computing curriculum and what this would look like in the classroom. I'm so pleased he was willing for I'm sure you will agree that for any primary colleague, the support and professional development he provides here has so much to explore, no matter where you are in your Computing confidence and expertise. He cites foundational sources of support and of course, if anyone is interested further in finding inspiration and resources to enhance the teaching and learning of Computing in your classroom or school, I'm sure that Allen would be more than willing to have conversations with you.

Reflecting on the voices of primary education

■ Which of the networks discussed by Allen have you not connected with yet?

_____

_____

_____

_____

_____

_____

■ What are some inquiry-based questions you could explore with your class over the next term?

_____

_____

_____

_____

_____

- What principles to develop children into proficient creators within technology will you implement into your class/school after reading Allen's discussion?

_____

_____

_____

_____

_____

_____

Integrating computing into the curriculum

Matt Roberts

I am extremely passionate about using computing skills to enhance experiences across the curriculum. When we consider Paul Watson's entry on children becoming creators, not consumers, the digital world is an ideal space to put that principle into practice. This will enable children who perhaps find it more difficult to put content knowledge into a written format easier to share what key concepts they are learning whilst at the same time developing their skills in using various forms of communication technology.

Impact on developing computing knowledge

Computing is an intriguing subject. It is often one that children are naturally drawn to because it utilises more and more technologies that our children have been aware of their entire lives. When they go home, they more often than not are given access to some form of computational technology. According to Ofcom (2022), 99% of all children and young people went online in 2021. With these statistics, there were some very worrying findings, thinking about children in primary education:

- A majority of children under 13 had their own profile on at least one social media app or site; 33% of parents of 5–7s said their child had a profile, and 60% of 8–11s said they had one.

- More than six in ten children aged 8–17 said they had more than one profile on some online apps and sites (62%); the most common reason, overall, was having one profile just for their parents, family or friends to see.

- More than a third (36%) of children aged 8–17 said they had seen something "worrying or nasty" online in the past 12 months; six in ten said they would always tell someone about this (59%).

Further:

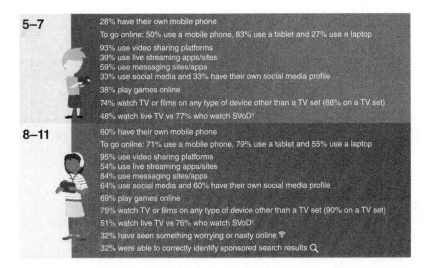

5–7

28% have their own mobile phone
To go online: 50% use a mobile phone, 83% use a tablet and 27% use a laptop
93% use video sharing platforms
39% use live streaming apps/sites
59% use messaging sites/apps
33% use social media and 33% have their own social media profile
38% play games online
74% watch TV or films on any type of device other than a TV set (88% on a TV set)
48% watch live TV vs 77% who watch SVoD¹

8–11

60% have their own mobile phone
To go online: 71% use a mobile phone, 79% use a tablet and 55% use a laptop
95% use video sharing platforms
54% use live streaming apps/sites
84% use messaging sites/apps
64% use social media and 60% have their own social media profile
69% play games online
79% watch TV or films on any type of device other than a TV set (90% on a TV set)
51% watch live TV vs 76% who watch SVoD¹
32% have seen something worrying or nasty online
32% were able to correctly identify sponsored search results

While these statistics are a useful reminder of how ubiquitous technology has become for those surveyed, their reliability might be questioned since watching YouTube videos is not the same as posting content to a channel that a child controls and operates. Primary-aged children (11 and under) must be reminded that companies that provide social media services such as video streaming or instant messaging are predominantly based in the US. Because of this, these companies follow US Federal law where the Children's Online Privacy Protection Act (1998) means for many social media providers, the minimum age for subscription or membership is 13. Primary or Elementary school teachers outside the US are unable to strictly enforce this age restriction. Instead, through active parental engagement, schools are recognising the practical benefits of being able to use these platforms safely and securely and are offering learning in Digital Citizenship to support this.

All of the above outlines the vital space that the Computing curriculum requires in our timetables. The reason for this is that Computing (since 2014) does not just cover how children create content, but the working behind that content and how to access it safely. These objectives can be broken down into three areas: Computing Science, Information Technology and Digital Literacy.

	KS1	**KS2**
CS	■ understand what algorithms are; how they are implemented as programs on digital devices; and that programs execute by following precise and unambiguous instructions ■ create and debug simple programs ■ use logical reasoning to predict the behaviour of simple programs	■ design, write and debug programs that accomplish specific goals, including controlling or simulating physical systems; solve problems by decomposing them into smaller parts ■ use sequence, selection and repetition in programs; work with variables and various forms of input and output ■ use logical reasoning to explain how some simple algorithms work and to detect and correct errors in algorithms and programs ■ understand computer networks including the Internet; how they can provide multiple services, such as the world wide web
IT	■ use technology purposefully to create, organise, store, manipulate and retrieve digital content	■ use search technologies effectively, appreciate how results are selected and ranked ■ select, use and combine a variety of software (including Internet services) on a range of digital devices to design and create a range of programs, systems and content that accomplish given goals, including collecting, analysing, evaluating and presenting data and information

(Continued)

	KS1	KS2
DL	■ recognise common uses of information technology beyond school ■ use technology safely and respectfully, keeping personal information private; identify here to go for help and support when they have concerns about content or contact on the Internet or other online technologies	■ understand the opportunities they offer for communication and collaboration ■ be discerning in evaluating digital content ■ use technology safely, respectfully and responsibly; recognise acceptable/unacceptable behaviour; identify a range of ways to report concerns about content and contact

(2014 Computing Programmes of Study)

The Computing Science aspects of the Computing curriculum are very much more subject-specific and the Digital Literacy would not look out of place linked with your PHSCE curriculum and in researching for any subject. However, it is the Information Technology (the type of things you would see in the ICT Curriculum pre-2014) that apply themselves so well to being developed through other subjects as an enhancement to help the children become creators using the key knowledge they are learning, not just passive consumers.

With the squeeze on the Primary timetable to fit in over a dozen subjects, it can be difficult to find ways to maximise learning for all subject areas without diminishing space needed for other subjects. Integrated Computing (at least the Information Technology strand of Computing) to enhance your study of wider curriculum areas helps to trim out more space for other subjects to develop the knowledge children need to acquire whilst using computing technology skills to embed the learning further. Black et al. (2013) identified that teachers felt that Computing needed to be made more relevant – helping our learners create real-life content is one way this can be done.

Impact on developing wider curriculum knowledge

Of course, if we are to consider including computing skills into wider areas of the curriculum, we must be sure that we are not diluting the content that our children should be gleaning in those subjects. If integrating technology into, say, History means that the attention and value are drawn away from the key historical knowledge, then it shouldn't be an option. However, it doesn't have to be like that.

In fact, utilising specific software to encourage children to present their learning or deepen their understanding of certain concepts will go a long way to developing learning in other curriculum areas. Not only can enhanced visuals and models be provided which are interactive but simply using the wide world connected through technology can provide motivation and enthusiasm to produce learning outcomes of the highest quality. For the remainder of this section, I hope to demonstrate just a few resources or ideas to implement into your classroom which are hopefully generic enough that they can be used with any year group or any subject. I have been inspired by the work of a number of great educators, such as Lee Parkinson (@ICT_MrP) in developing these ideas and have drawn on them in considering how I can apply some of these excellent examples to my own classroom practice.

Integrating computing examples

Connect with real-life inspirations

Before diving into specific ideas and platforms that can be used to enhance the way knowledge and skills can be applied across the curriculum using technology, I want to spotlight the thing that sets using technology apart from any other source of media – the ability to publish and share it instantly anywhere in the world. When I was in education myself, the best I could hope for was that my teacher could somehow get in touch with an author or organisation through the post, create photocopies of my work and send it off which in itself would be a time-heavy burden on my teacher as well as a lot more difficult to plan ahead to do as the communication would have to happen weeks, sometimes maybe even months, before creating my content in the class.

Now, we have the power in this digital age to make contact within seconds to any possible source of inspiration out there! You want to send some examples of children's writing based on an author's book to them – easy. You want to share your presentations on the importance of raising awareness about climate change with your local environmental agency – no problem. You want to publish your debates about an important historical figure with the local museum – it's just a few clicks away! The world really is your class' platform with the technology they have at their fingertips. Of course, it will require a little online networking from yourself but hopefully this will not be too difficult and many individuals and organisations love linking up with schools to spread their message and vision out further. You never know, your class' work may be used in their future materials!

Just a few examples of this that I have carried out include mainly linking with children's authors. We have had some lovely messages back, and one author even created a three-minute video thanking my class for their hard work and even reciting some phrases that she loved and may use in her future writing! The fact that she mentioned "Mr Roberts" blew their minds!

Using green screen software to publish real content

Green screens are really only something I've started to use within the last academic year. I have seen the power that they hold with others using them but never quite gotten into it myself. However, when a dinosaur appeared at the beginning of COP26 urging mankind to not bring about their own extinction, I had to sit up and think a bit more about how we could bring a discussion to life about this in our class.

We gathered all the information we could about climate change, COP26 and what the plans were after this landmark conference to help reduce the damage we are doing to the Earth's atmosphere. We used a newsroom backdrop, located scenes to insert in the background which demonstrate the impact of climate change on the planet and then the children were able to publish short videos which highlight the importance of raising the awareness of climate change. Of course, when I explained that using green screens would be how their favourite YouTubers would create their videos with effects and backdrops, they were instantly intrigued!

We could have produced written non-chronological reports or double-page spreads. However, the children in my class who struggle more with writing their ideas were able to flourish because they could explain what they had been learning verbally and create content which engaged their viewers more.

Again, this tool can be used with any topic and if you have younger year groups who would struggle to use apps such as *Do Ink Green Screen*, for example (the one I used), you can just get them to record the videos and ask a willing Y6 volunteer to put it together for you. Honestly, they taught me a few tricks as we were putting this content together!

Animation to bring life to their education

If the focus of the learning is to explain a scientific process or deliver knowledge about a historical event, why not create an animated film to help you do this. Children will be able to bring their ideas to life and will enthusiastically craft clear and concise explanations, using technical vocabulary, if their final "piece" is to become part of an animated video which can then be shared onto places like YouTube. Again, the barrier of having to write the information will be removed and children can work towards producing work that can be shared and interacted with in the wider world – becoming creators, not just consumers as, again, so excellently put by Paul Watson.

What next?

Above, I have outlined just a few possible ideas on how you not only make your Computing sessions more focused but also increase the time your class have engaging with wider curriculum content and retrieving that knowledge to use in a purposeful way to produce their own content which they will be proud to share. There are far more possibilities with integrating technology into the wider curriculum, but I hope that this piece has given you a rationale behind this approach and given you some starting points.

Along with all the suggestions for the classroom above, there is a wide world out there of professional development and guidance for the teaching of computing and other curriculum areas.

For example, the Computing at School network is a community of teachers supported by the BCS, the chartered Institute for IT, who have a wealth of experience teaching across all age ranges from pre-schoolers to University. Many of those teachers have offered to share their expertise for free or at relatively low cost to subscribe to their publications. The formation of the National Centre for Computing Education in 2018 by a consortium of the National STEM Learning Centre with the Raspberry Pi Foundation and

BCS, funded by the Department for Education, went a step further by developing a whole programme from KS1 to KS4 of resources for teaching Computing. The National Centre for Computing Education also offered a certification programme to enable Primary and Secondary teachers to develop their subject knowledge and pedagogical expertise to global standards. If you are seeking to further your knowledge in this subject area, there is so much to connect with out there!

Reflecting on the voices of primary education

- How confident are you at using technology in the classroom to create a wider array of content with your class?

- Which topic area coming up do you see a potential in to create content using technology with your class?

■ What tools/technologies are you less familiar with that you can find out more about?

_____

_____

_____

_____

_____

_____

References

Black, J., Brodie, J., Curzon, P., Myketiak, C., McOwan, P. W., & Meagher, L. R. (2013). Making Computing interesting to school students. Proceedings of the 18th ACM Conference on Innovation and Technology in Computer Science Education (ITiCSE '13). Canterbury, UK. 255.

Ofcom. (2022). Children and Parents: Media Use and Attitudes Report, 2022.

10

Well-being and keeping fresh as a teacher

Paul Hume – @TeacherPaul1978
Kate Aspin – @etaknipsa

Placing this chapter at the end at first did not sit right with me. Nevertheless, making sure our well-being is healthy and that we are keeping invigorated in what can be a very draining profession is probably the most important thing that will be spoken about in this book. However, maybe that is why it should be at the end. Despite all the outstanding ideas, the inspirational submitters and the innovative practice to try and implement, the biggest thing to take away from this book is how we should be looking after ourselves and remember that there is more to life than this wonderful vocation that we have chosen to embark on. So yes, take away some excellent ideas from the previous chapters, come back to their thoughts and ideas over time … but most importantly take in the thoughts from this final chapter and reflect on how you can take better care of yourself.

To begin with, Paul Hume will share what he ingeniously calls his "Health Care Plan" – HCP. Each letter stands for something specific that he believes if you keep track of and make sure you are keeping well too, and then you will be a lot happier and healthier in every way. Kate Aspin, who has trained numerous trainee teachers, will then share one of the excellent analogies that she brought to the podcast and go more in-depth about how we need to stay as grapes when we go about our teaching and not become raisins!

DOI: 10.4324/9781003307150-10

Finding your Health Care Plan

Paul Hume

When I reflect on my experience, I can see how every hurdle, obstacle and speed bump have moulded me into the leader I am today. My understanding of what leadership is has also changed. As a newly qualified teacher (NQT), I had a determined ambition to be a leader, not fully realising that I already was – a teacher; a role model to children. I giggle when I think back to myself pasting the wall behind my desk with the Excellent Teacher Standards and post-it noting everything I was doing to meet them … as an NQT … lol! But my core values have always been there.

I have learned a lot of lessons along the way and developed a set of core values – my HCP, my Health Care Plan – which I hope will inspire you to find yours. This brings me to my HCP. Core values that shape my teaching and leadership actions and help me to be the best that I can be. Honesty, capacity, preparation – my Health Care Plan.

Honesty

This is about being honest with yourself and everyone around you: children, colleagues, family, friends, etc. It's about realising when you need help and reaching out for it. It's also about knowing what you are capable of doing and believing in what you are capable of achieving. I thought I knew myself, but I got to know myself even more when I began mentoring. In a way, it refined my practice and actually made me realise what I had to offer, not from arrogance as when I began my journey, the experience was drawing it out of me, revealing it, like a soul mirror. I had a great mentor to look back on, to inspire my actions. Suddenly, I had a teacher who was relying on me. I learned that I was compassionate, that I was a good listener, that I was reflective, that I could deliver clear lessons, that I was a good role model and that I was a good team player. Qualities I used to take for granted early on, or worse, not bring out in others.

Honesty.

Some honesty questions to reflect on:

Who are you? What are your talents? How can they be used to further the achievement and success of your children and colleagues? What are your weaknesses? Know that within those weaknesses are opportunities for great success and growth.

Tips:

Keep reflecting back on the teacher's standards. Identify your strengths and weaknesses.

Take part in conversations. Join in with edu-Twitter communities. You'll soon be not only finding help but also giving help and support, which helps us all to be more honest with ourselves and others.

Treat all with equity and kindness. It's hard sometimes but positivity feeds positivity.

Capacity

This is about your limits. Your capacity. It links to honesty, as knowing your capacity empowers you to say stop when you know you've reached your limit. On the other hand, this is about knowing how much more you can achieve. That you have capacity for greatness. That your capacity in this sense can be increased. Surrounding yourself with the right people ensures that your capacity is fulfilled. When I joined Twitter, I started with #MTPMonday, #TinyVoiceTalks and #FFBWednesday. I wanted to connect with other teachers. What I didn't anticipate was meeting so many positive people who inspire and challenge me every day. Now #MorningTom, #YourMindMatters, #kindnessripple and my own #FYFlamingoF help to keep the positivity flowing. But there's a humble part of me that doubts I could ever be like the leaders that I follow. I feel in awe. I feel humble. And that is why I know that they are the right people to surround myself with. They spread kindness.

Choose your battles! I learned not to fight over every tedious point, but I will challenge practices that are damaging to well-being. In one school, teachers asked that I become their phase leader. Here was the turning point in my understanding of leadership. It wasn't from my own pursuit but arose from the needs and welfare of others; just as we do for our children. My journey has not been plain-sailing. I have found my way into senior leadership not from wanting it as I used to, but from where the need has arisen. I've been in the right place at the right time with the right set of qualities, the latter being key. I am reminded of my past and it gives me strength, but also doubt. I doubt that I can do it, that I'm not ready. So different from the arrogant NQT 13 years ago. What do I know? Well, I do know my heart, and I know what I have to offer. There is more to learn, yes, and that is where I find hope.

When all is said and done, you might have strong ambitions, bags of experience and self-confidence; however without kindness and love, the journey is futile.

Be careful and watch out for those who are a drain on your capacity. Let them go.

So: what is your capacity? Who is draining your capacity? Are you allowing it to be drained? Can you say stop so that you don't overflow? Are the right people around you contributing to a fulfilled capacity?

Tips:

Keep a list! Prioritise those jobs that must be done now and set other tasks aside to be completed later.

Preparation

A few years ago, I burned myself out (marking way too much, over-planning, not taking any time for well-being), and had to step away for a while. I was trying to be prepared but achieving the opposite. Eventually, this dark period redefined my attitude to workload and where I learned the value of live marking – marking as you circulate, giving verbal feedback; that children can draw their own tables in their books, write their own dates, draw their own Venn diagrams, I could go on; that asking for help is not a weakness – recognising the value of the team. I also make sure I leave early one day for my well-being – to run, meet up with friends or go to a movie. I read up on the union's workload guidance and that became my authority. I would never again allow the bureaucracy and administration to ruin what I knew was the vocation I was called to do.

While preparation is key to successful lessons, this is also about being prepared for the role you are undertaking. Are you ready? Go back to the start of the day. Have you prepared yourself with the right sustenance? Did you get enough sleep? Does your diet prepare you to be the best physically and mentally? Do your friends, hobbies and social life prepare you to be the best (relating to honesty and capacity)? Do you exercise enough to be as prepared as you can be?

Moving on to continuous professional development (CPD). What courses, books or articles could you take part in or read to keep you better prepared? Do you anticipate problems so that you are prepared for them? This could be lessons or in general.

Tips:

Set aside a day each week that you will leave early.

Drink plenty of water!

Go to bed early so that you can switch off/read/listen to music before sleeping – getting enough sleep helps in so many ways.

Introduce yoga/meditation into your routine. Even 10 minutes can have a positive impact. I use Kelly Howell guided meditations, and the free Nike Training App has lots of great yoga sessions for all abilities.

I do try to follow my own advice as much as possible and there are days when I fail. However, because I am honest with myself and that I know my capacity, I can at least make some changes so that I am better prepared when I face these problems again.

What is your Health Care Plan?

When Paul and I met together for our Primary Education Voices chat, I was so pleased to hear about his Primary Three – which formed the HCP that he has outlined above. Paul's leadership is clearly focused on the well-being of the staff in his school and this has come from clear personal experience as he listed above.

With his thoughts, I am so grateful that he has given distinct tips and questions to help guide our practice. The reality is that when we are not taking care of our own health and well-being then we will be less effective and productive in the classroom. No amount of evidence-informed practice, quality first teaching and targeted interventions can have a sustained, positive impact on teaching and learning in the classroom unless the classroom practitioner is in the right frame of mind, feeling comfortable in themselves or indeed in the actual classroom because they are feeling well enough to be so! In this book, there has been a host of useful tips, incredible pieces of advice and excellent research cited into how we can develop our practice but all of the previous sections would not be possible without ensuring that we are taking care of ourselves.

Paul's suggestions are excellent as a starting point but, of course, your own well-being activities and avenues will be guided by your own life, circumstances and preferences. Use the questions he suggests and the spaces below to consider how you can keep yourself prepared to move forward in this profession.

Reflecting on the voices of primary education

■ What steps can you take to recognise your Capacity in your practice?

_____

_____

_____

_____

_____

■ What steps can you take to develop Honesty to yourself in your practice?

_____

_____

_____

_____

_____

> ■ What steps can you take to incorporate Preparation in your practice?
>
> _____
>
> _____
>
> _____
>
> _____
>
> _____

Grapes and raisins – A teacher's journey...

Kate Aspin

When you think of a grape, what comes to mind? Juice? Colours and flavours? Sweetness? Succulent? Adjectives tend to imply a fulsome taste experience bursting with juicy delights.

In my work with trainees, novices and new teachers, I notice a similarity between them and grapes; they can be bursting with energy and enthusiasm, delighting in the new things they notice about children and learning, a desire to make a difference, an impact. This "juiciness" rubs off on myself and others, we see the teaching world through renewed eyes, appreciating the joy when a child "gets it" and light bulb moments occur.

However, with all teachers at some point in their teaching journey, the joy and the juice begin to ebb slightly. All it takes is a knock here, criticism there, public opinions vented (especially via social media), parental gripes, Ofsted downward pressure and toxic management, one or many of these happen on a regular basis in many schools. All of these can, over time, make a teacher feel deflated and frustrated, wearing away the skin on the grape and causing the juice to leak out.

Many of us do not notice this to being with, too busy getting on with the job, shrugging it off and cracking on. Eventually, however, it takes its toll physically and mentally and we gradually shrivel and dry up, losing sight of the original reasons we came to into teaching. We start to "raisin," lose our sweet succulence, and start to reflect differently on the role, becoming more cynical and can scoff at the naive new grapes as they appear in the staff room.

What can we do then, to "re-grape" ourselves, to reconnect with our original drive and passion for the role? Some people don't and move out of teaching and into other work and roles, this is fine if it is a choice freely taken. But what if you wish to reinvigorate and inject their teaching with fresh juice? What can you do if you feel yourself becoming a "raisin"?

The first thing is to recognise that you need to make a change. This can be difficult as teaching takes time to bed-in and gradually becomes natural, resourced, planned and the year group we are currently in more and more comfortable. You know your school, the routine and year pattern, when it is your turn for assemblies and performances. Making a change takes courage because, inevitably it will mean more work, a new cognitive load and a risk to take and this takes courage.

However, to grow we need to try new things to make changes. Change is inevitable within schools; it is the one thing we can depend upon. However, many of the changes we face are given from above, we have no say. When we decide to make our own changes, this is our decision which is reinvigorating.

So what might you change that will help you be "more grape"?

Firstly, a change in year group is worth considering. If you have been in your year group or key stage for a long time, the subject knowledge and the associated misconceptions become naturalised to you and you know exactly what happens when and why. This is comforting but also can become mechanistic and dare I say, boring. A change of year group, especially a drastic change perhaps of key stage, will challenge you mentally and physically and make you think differently about your school and the whole journey of a primary child. This is especially great if you are considering school leadership in the future, seeing more of the whole school's viewpoint. If you are thinking about this, ask your leadership if you can spend time in another part of the school, observe an experienced colleague or do a swap perhaps take the year group for a term in your particular subject specialism. They could, in turn, take your class for theirs. This is productive in various ways, you both get to know another class well and get a "flavour" of a different phase, out of your comfort zone. You also get to deepen and extend your own subject knowledge and pedagogical knowledge regarding teaching your subject specialism, which can only improve your understanding and give you greater credibility amongst the staff in that phase. I did this myself, swapping my own class for music with another where I took the PE; this played to our teaching strengths and enabled me to explore a different age phase, gently.

Another strategy you could try if moving year group feels a bit drastic is to ask to change curriculum responsibility. Most primary staff, especially if recruited as a new teacher, are given a subject to lead, regardless of interest or talent or knowledge. After a while, if you have a real passion for a subject and a vacancy arises with a subject it is a great way to reinvigorate yourself. If you are in a large school it may be that you could shadow another member of staff or even split the subject into EYFS/KS1 and KS2 responsibilities. I strongly recommend engaging with the numerous subject associations that exist to support curriculum leadership now. These used to be very secondary orientated in focus but have changed recently and can really support personal subject knowledge development and help subject leaders plan and structure their curriculum. A new subject may reignite and reinvigorate your "juices."

Something else worth considering is to engage more with the wider aspects of school life, so gaining experience as an initial teacher training (ITT) or early career teacher (ECT) mentor. This can involve seeing teaching from a fresh direction, looking at your class from another perspective and engaging with current thinking and new approaches. It will remind you of your own journey, how far you have come and that you really do know what you are doing! Working in concert with a good trainee is a truly joyful experience, moving your children forward together. Turning around a struggling trainee can also be very satisfying; helping them to unpick and rebuild areas can make you reflect anew on your own development. If you are interested in this and beyond your ECT years then speak to your leadership and then to your local training providers, they will be able to offer you support and training. Coaching and mentoring is a growth area in schools currently and a very rewarding one, and working with a trainee can be a fantastic starting point for growth.

Becoming the staff governor of the governing body may also be an invigorating challenge. Understanding the bigger picture of the school structure, where decisions stem from and the complexity of policy and finance can really help understand some of the frustrations that class teachers can face when they feel things are being done to rather than with them. It gives a fresh perspective. I did this myself and became the staff governor, it was an interesting role where I grew and deepened my understanding of school systems. I had been a teacher for a few years at that point, in two different schools and, at times had been exasperated by decisions and reasons for change within the school. I realised that it was the "bigger picture" where I was lacking. As a governor, you understand more about the legislation and rationale for decisions as well as key aspects such as the budget. As a class teacher, the "budget" tend to be a mythical thing that gets mentioned in staff meetings and has connotations of "tightening belts" and the word no. Once you understand governance you have a better view of the school as a whole and where decisions emerge from. It does not always make them any more palatable but you have a handle on the wider issues. This is great for all staff, especially if you are considering a move into leadership.

Finally, the biggest change you can make to reinvigorate and "re-grape" is to change school. This is a big gamble as you are really going to have to come out of your comfort zone; leave the staff, friends and connections that you have carefully honed and the credibility you had with families and children. However, trying a bigger/smaller/more diverse school may be just the tonic you need. You will experience a range of emotions and you will feel yourself asking why you left, why what you did at X school was better/different but you will settle in and have new challenges and new connections, allow yourself the time for this, do not pressure yourself at the start. Your teacher "grape" will initially take a hit as the cognitive load of a new setting is huge, but the sense of growth as you bed in will be a real tonic.

Whatever you decide to do, keeping your inner grape juicy will mean the job will remain enjoyable for your whole teaching career!

When Kate laid out this grape and raisin analogy in our discussion, I knew it would be one that I would have to take with me along my path through Primary Education. I think the power of it is the sense that I'm sure every teacher could relate to this along their progression through the profession. In my own journey, I can now look back at almost a decade of teaching experience and see the times where I was most certainly a raisin and was just going through the motions.

One particular moment in time saw me dealing with a child who was by far the most challenging I had to work with as a teacher. Whilst I was certainly receiving support by my senior leaders in this difficulty, I was struggling. To those I worked with, I would put on a happy, coping exterior but deep down I was drying up. For some reason, my work was keeping me up past midnight on a regular basis when I hadn't been before – something I look back on now and realise that this was probably down to me begrudging my work and worrying about what the next day would bring. For many teachers, the trigger of these types of pressure will vary but what is important is that we don't lose sight of what made us fall in love with teaching in the first place. From dozens and dozens of podcast interviews, it is clear that those things we fall in love with about teaching also differ.

For me, the thing that revitalised my teaching juices was a change in curriculum leadership – something with Kate referred to in her discussion. I was given the opportunity to take the lead on Maths in my three-form entry school which had been a desire of mine from my time as a trainee teacher. This role challenged me in different ways, gave me opportunities to work with the senior leadership team and I found new enthusiasm in my role. I was also given the opportunity to teach Maths to both Year 6 classes whilst my year partner taught writing, meaning I was focusing on an area that I felt I had more expertise in, as Kate suggested. Whilst some may argue it may have "de-skilled" me, I felt alleviated of having to plan, teach and assess two vital curriculum areas with my class and focus on one with both classes. It also gave me a brief respite from working with that particular child. It was the ideal tonic for that circumstance. I am not saying that this is the solution for your scenario if you are feeling a bit "raisiny," but it shows that the answer does not have to be to leave the profession entirely. If you are going through a "raisin phase," I'm sure you will find wise guidance in Kate's words.

Reflecting on the voices of primary education

- Why are you a teacher, and what is keeping you in the role of a teacher?

_____

_____

_____

_____

_____

_____

- What are the best thing and the worst thing about your current role?

_____

_____

_____

_____

_____

_____

- What can you change from now about your role and what is holding you back?

_____

_____

_____

_____

_____

_____

Index